Foundations

The School Mathematics Project

*The right of the
University of Cambridge
to print and sell
all manner of books
was granted by
Henry VIII in 1534.
The University has printed
and published continuously
since 1584.*

Cambridge University Press

Cambridge   New York   Port Chester   Melbourne   Sydney

Main authors	Simon Baxter
	Stan Dolan
	Doug French
	Andy Hall
	Barrie Hunt
	Lorna Lyons

Team leader   Barri

Project director   Stan

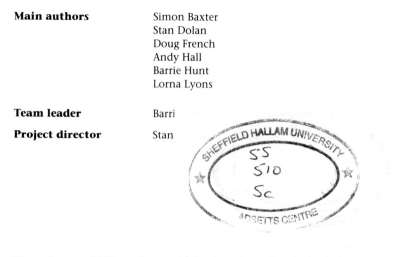

The authors would like to give special thanks to Ann White for her help in producing the trial edition and in preparing this book for publication.

The publishers would like to thank the following for supplying photographs:

page 36 – Tony Duffy/All Sport Photographic Ltd;
page 37 – Horst H. Baumann/ZEFA;
page 38 – Chris Raphael/ All Sport Photographic Ltd;
page 104 – The Ancient Art and Architecture Collection
          (Ronald Sheridan's Photo Library);
page 113 – David Thompson/Oxford Scientific Films;
page 116 – The Ancient Art and Architecture Collection
          (Ronald Sheridan's Photo Library).

Cover design by Iguana Creative Design

Cartoons by Tony Hall

Published by the Press Syndicate of the University of Cambridge
The Pitt Building, Trumpington Street, Cambridge CB2 1RP
40 West 20th Street, New York, NY 10011–4211, USA
10 Stamford Road, Oakleigh, Victoria 3166, Australia

First published 1991
Reprinted 1992

Produced by Gecko Limited, Bicester, Oxon

Printed in Great Britain at the University Press, Cambridge

British Library cataloguing in publication data
16–19 Mathematics.
Foundations.
Student's text
1. Mathematics
I. School Mathematics Project
515

ISBN 0 521 38842 2

Contents

1 Graphs

1.1 Introduction

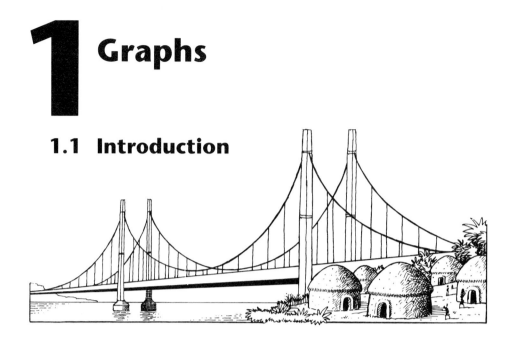

Many fascinating curves occur in nature and in manufactured structures. Mud huts from central Africa are constructed in a quadratic form so that they are lightweight and stable, whilst the central curve of the modern suspension bridge is strong and elegant.

This chapter is concerned with the use of graph sketching in problem-solving. Graphical approaches often help us to see how to proceed. This is illustrated in example 1.

EXAMPLE 1

A market trader finds that she can sell 60 transistor radios each week if she reduces her profit margin to zero, but sales drop when she increases her price. In fact, at £6.00 profit per radio she sells none at all. What profit margin should she choose to achieve the greatest possible total profit?

SOLUTION

To help decide what profit margin to choose, the trader models her sales figures with the straight-line graph shown:

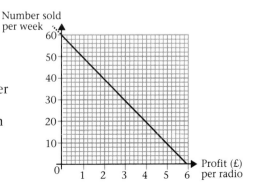

(a) Use the graph to copy and complete this table.

Profit (£) per radio	0	1	2	3	4	5	6
Number of radios sold		60					0
Total profit (£) from sales						50	

(b) Draw a graph from this table, plotting total profit against profit per radio. (The solution to the trader's problem should now be quite easy to see.)

(c) What profit per radio should she choose?

Suppose the profit is £x per radio.

(a) Find the number of radios that the trader sells per week in terms of x.

(b) What is her total profit from sales in terms of x?

(c) What are the equations of the straight-line graph in example 1 and the graph that you have drawn?

Practical problems can lead to many different types of graph. Example 1 used a straight line and a curve. Tasksheet 1 looks at more graphs and their equations.

TASKSHEET 1 – Investigating curves (page 18)

In sections 1.2 and 1.3 you will study graphs like those used in example 1.

1.2 Linear graphs

When a function has a straight-line graph, it is said to be **linear**.

Examples of straight-line graphs may be found in a wide range of subjects.

(a) The distance against time graph of a body moving with constant speed is a straight line.

(b) Economists often assume that the demand for a commodity decreases linearly with price, as in example 1.

(c) The amount by which a metal rod expands when it is heated is proportional to its temperature and so the graph of length against temperature is linear.

Linear graphs are simple to deal with. Sometimes you can approximate more complex graphs by linear graphs, as in example 2.

E X A M P L E   2

A long-distance walker aims to cover the 800 miles from John O'Groats to Land's End at the rate of 30 miles per day.

The graphs below illustrate his progress after *t* days.

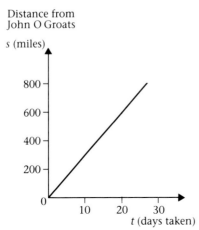

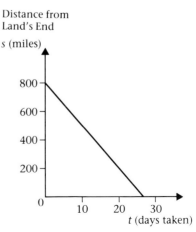

(a) What distance has the walker covered after one day and how far is he from Land's End?

(b) How far has he walked after two days and how far is he from Land's End?

(c) How far has he walked after t days and how far is he from Land's End?

(d) What are the equations of the two graphs of distance against time?

What assumptions have been made to obtain straight-line graphs? Do you think these assumptions are reasonable?

Both graphs have the following features:

- Both are straight-line or **linear** graphs. For this reason $30t$ and $800 - 30t$ are called **linear functions** of t.

- The graph of $s = 30t$ passes through the origin and has a **gradient** of 30.

- The graph of $s = 800 - 30t$ crosses the s-axis at 800. The number 800 is called the **intercept** on the s-axis. This function is decreasing, the graph having a **negative gradient** of -30.

An introduction to straight-line graphs is provided in supplementary tasksheet 2S.

T A S K S H E E T 2S – The equation of a straight line (page 19)

> y is a **linear function** of x if it can be expressed in the form $mx + c$.
>
> The graph of y against x is then a straight line.
>
> m is the **gradient** of the line.
>
> c is the value of y when x is zero and is the **intercept** on the y-axis.

There are a number of ways of finding the equation of a line if you know a couple of points on the line.

> How would you find the equation of the straight line through (1, 2) and (3, 8)?

A method which is quick and easy to use is illustrated in example 3.

E X A M P L E 3

Find the equation of the straight line through (1, 2) and (3, 8).

S O L U T I O N

Gradient $= \dfrac{y - 2}{x - 1}$

or

Gradient $= \dfrac{6}{2} = 3$

With practice it is possible to write down

$$\frac{y - 2}{x - 1} = \frac{6}{2}$$

$$\Rightarrow y - 2 = 3(x - 1) \qquad (\Rightarrow \text{means 'implies'})$$

> (a) Do different methods give the same equation?
>
> (b) Show that using $\dfrac{y - 8}{x - 3}$ as the gradient gives the same equation.

E X E R C I S E   1

1 Draw the straight lines

(a) $y = 2x + 4$ (b) $s = -2t + 7$ (c) $2y = 4x - 3$

(d) $x = -y + 4$ (e) $y = 5$ (f) $x = 3$

2 Write down the equation for each of the following straight lines.

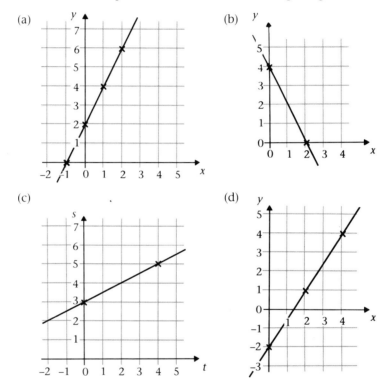

(a)

(b)

(c)

(d)

3 Find the equations of the straight lines passing through the points

(a) (0, 3) and (2, 7)   (b) (1, 4) and (2, 6)

(c) (1, −5) and (−4, 0)   (d) (1, 2) and (−2, 1)

4 Which of the following equations have straight-line graphs?

(a) $y = x^2 - 2$ (b) $2y + x = 4$ (c) $x^2 + y^2 = 9$

(d) $xy = 5$ (e) $x = 5 - 2y$ (f) $x - y = 2x - y + 6$

(g) $y - 3 = 4(x + 1)$ (h) $\dfrac{x}{2} + \dfrac{y}{3} = 1$ (i) $\sqrt{y} = \sqrt{x} + 1$

1.3 Quadratic functions

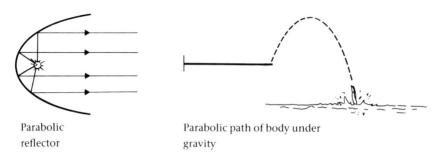

Parabolic
reflector

Parabolic path of body under
gravity

You can see the curve known as a **parabola** in various everyday situations and it arises in mathematics most simply as the graph $y = x^2$.

The curve has line symmetry in the y-axis and a **vertex** at the origin. In this case the vertex is the minimum point. For inverted parabolas it would be the maximum point.

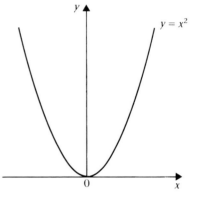

Polynomial functions of x are functions formed by adding together powers of x.

Examples are $3x + 1$

$x^2 + 5x - 2$

$5x^4 - 3x^3 + 2x^2 + 7x - 5$

(Note: the powers of x must be non-negative whole numbers.)

You have already looked at linear functions where the highest power of x present is the first power, x^1 (or just x). In this section you will look at **quadratic functions** of the form

$$y = ax^2 + bx + c \quad (a \neq 0)$$

where the highest power is x^2. If $a = 0$, then this is a linear function.

(a) Use a graph plotter to plot the function

$$y = ax^2$$

for various positive, negative and fractional values of a. What do you notice?

(b) Plot the function

$$y = ax^2 + bx + c$$

for various positive, negative and fractional values of a, b and c. (You will need to vary one coefficient at a time, keeping the others constant.) What do you notice?

Tasksheets 3 and 3E look at some of the simplest transformations of $y = x^2$ and find that $y = ax^2 + bx + c$ is not always the most helpful form of the equation of a quadratic function.

T A S K S H E E T   3   O R   3 E – *Translations of the quadratic curve (pages 22 and 24)*

For the rest of this chapter we shall concentrate on quadratics of the form $x^2 + bx + c$ (i.e. $a = 1$).

> The graph of $y = (x + p)^2 + q$ is a translation of the graph
>
> of $y = x^2$ through the vector $\begin{bmatrix} -p \\ q \end{bmatrix}$.

E X A M P L E   4

$(x + 3)(x + 3)$

$x^2 + 6x + 9$ –

Sketch the graph of $y = (x + 3)^2 - 7$.

$= x^2 + 3x + 3x + 9$

S O L U T I O N

The graph of $y = (x + 3)^2 - 7$ is obtained by translating the

graph of $y = x^2$ through $\begin{bmatrix} -3 \\ -7 \end{bmatrix}$.

As the vertex of $y = x^2$ is at $(0, 0)$, you can see that the vertex of $y = (x + 3)^2 - 7$ is at $(-3, -7)$.

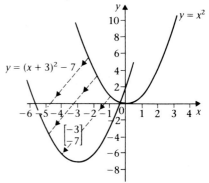

1.4 Completing the square

You have just found that $y = (x + p)^2 + q$ is an alternative form of the function $y = x^2 + bx + c$. We shall now investigate how to change between the two forms.

You may find it helpful to revise how to multiply brackets quickly and easily, and in particular how to calculate squares.

TASKSHEET 4S – Multiplying brackets (page 25)

EXAMPLE 5

Multiply out $(x + 5)(x - 3)$

SOLUTION

$$(x + 5)(x - 3) = x(x - 3) + 5(x - 3)$$
$$= x^2 - 3x + 5x - 15$$
$$= x^2 + 2x - 15$$

With practice you should be able to write down the answer straight away.

$(\overset{\frown}{x + 5})(x - 3)$ gives x^2

$(x + 5)(x - 3)$ gives $2x$ which combine to give $x^2 + 2x - 15$.

$(x + 5)(x - 3)$ gives -15

TASKSHEET 5 OR 5E – Completing the square
(pages 26 and 27)

Writing $x^2 + bx + c$ in the form $(x + p)^2 + q$ is known as **completing the square**.

In order to complete the square on $x^2 + bx + c$

(a) write $x^2 + bx$ in the form $(x + p)^2 + q$

    where $p = \frac{1}{2}b$ and $q = -p^2$,

(b) adjust the constant term by adding on c.

E X A M P L E   6

Complete the square on $x^2 + 6x + 2$.

S O L U T I O N

$$\text{halve} \quad \text{square}$$

$$x^2 + 6x = (x + 3)^2 - 9$$

$$x^2 + 6x + 2 = (x + 3)^2 - 9 + 2$$

$$x^2 + 6x + 2 = (x + 3)^2 - 7$$

E X E R C I S E   2

1   For each of the following equations

    (a) $y = x^2 + 8x + 5$ (b) $y = x^2 - 4x - 3$

    (c) $y = x^2 - 5x + 6$ (d) $y = x^2 - 7x - 3$

      (i) complete the square;

      (ii) check your answer by multiplying out;

      (iii) without using a graph plotter, sketch the corresponding graph.

2   (a) Write down a possible completed square form for the quadratic functions whose graphs are shown below.

    (b) Hence write down the equations of the quadratic functions in the form $y = x^2 + bx + c$.

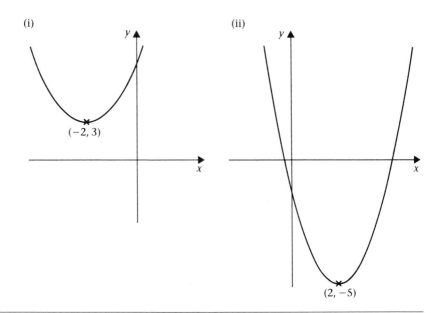

(i)

$(-2, 3)$

(ii)

$(2, -5)$

1.5 Zeros of quadratics

The axis of symmetry and the vertex of the parabola are important features of the graph, but they are by no means the only ones. Also useful are the points at which the graph crosses the axes, if it does! The graphs of all quadratic functions must cross the y-axis, but some graphs, such as those below, do not cross the x-axis.

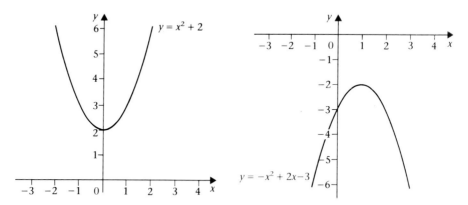

For the graph of any function, the point of intersection with the y-axis is easily found by putting $x=0$ in the function. The values of x at the points of intersection with the x-axis are called the **roots** of the equation $y=0$, and are also known as the **zeros** of the function because they make the function equal to zero. The zeros of $x^2 - x - 6$ are -2 and 3.

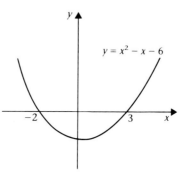

(a) If a product of two numbers ab equals 0, what can you say about either a or b?

(b) State all solutions of

   (i) $x + 2 = 0$ (ii) $x - 1 = 0$ (iii) $(x - 1)(x + 2) = 0$

T A S K S H E E T *6 – Factorised quadratics (page 29)*

Sketching a quadratic

You have seen that a quadratic function in expanded form such as

$$x^2 + 6x + 5$$

may also be expressed in completed square form

$$(x + 3)^2 - 4 \qquad (x + 3)(x + 3)$$

or in factorised form

$$(x + 1)(x + 5)$$

The zeros of $(x + 1)(x + 5)$ are the roots of $(x + 1)(x + 5) = 0$ and are found by putting $x + 1 = 0$ and $x + 5 = 0$ to give $x = -1$ and $x = -5$.

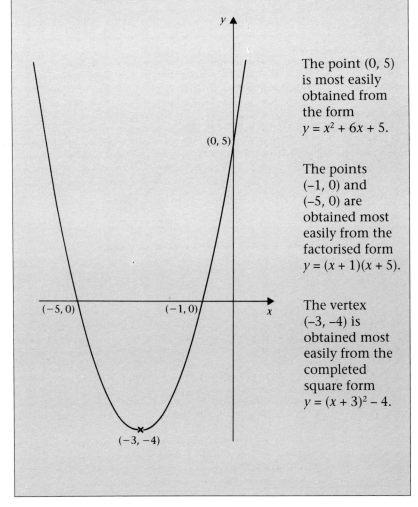

The point $(0, 5)$ is most easily obtained from the form $y = x^2 + 6x + 5$.

The points $(-1, 0)$ and $(-5, 0)$ are obtained most easily from the factorised form $y = (x + 1)(x + 5)$.

The vertex $(-3, -4)$ is obtained most easily from the completed square form $y = (x + 3)^2 - 4$.

1.6 **Factorising quadratics**

To find where the graph of a quadratic function crosses the x-axis it is helpful to have the quadratic expression in a factorised form such as $(x + 1)(x + 5)$. You must therefore be able to factorise the form $ax^2 + bx + c$ whenever this is possible. Initially we shall only consider examples with $a = 1$.

> (a) Explain why $x + 2$ is a possible factor of $x^2 - x - 12$, yet $x - 5$ could not be a factor.
>
> (b) Give all twelve possible factors of $x^2 - x - 12$.
>
> (c) Factorise $x^2 - x - 12$.

TASKSHEET 7S – Further factorisation (page 31)

The relationships illustrated for the quadratic $x^2 - 9x + 18$ enable you to factorise quadratic expressions which have integer roots.

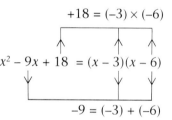

$$+18 = (-3) \times (-6)$$

$$x^2 - 9x + 18 = (x - 3)(x - 6)$$

$$-9 = (-3) + (-6)$$

EXERCISE 3

1 Factorise the following. You may check your answers by using a graph plotter to plot the graphs of each of the two forms.

(a) $x^2 + 7x + 12$ (b) $x^2 - 2x - 3$ (c) $x^2 - 7x + 10$

(d) $x^2 - 4$ (e) $x^2 - 7x$ (f) $x^2 - 6x + 9$

(g) $x^2 + 3x + 2$ (h) $x^2 + 4x + 4$ (i) $x^2 - 49$

2 Use a graph plotter to plot the graphs of

(a) $y = x^2 + 3x + 2$ (b) $y = x^2 + x - 1$ (c) $y = x^2 - x + 1$

In each case determine whether

(i) the quadratic function has any zeros;

(ii) the quadratic expression can be factorised.

After working through this chapter you should:

1 be able to find the gradient and the equation of a line joining two points;

2 be familiar with linear functions and the equations of straight lines;

3 be able to translate the graph of $y = x^2$ and find the equation of its image;

4 know how to complete the square to find the position of the vertex and the equation of the line of symmetry for the graph of a quadratic function;

5 be able to find, when possible, the zeros of a quadratic function from the factorised form;

6 know how to rewrite one form of the quadratic into any other using the scheme outlined below.

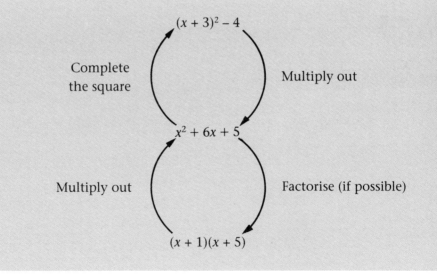

Investigating curves

1 Use a graph plotter to draw each of the following basic functions and their graphs. Sketch them and note any features which you think are interesting. Help is given on Technology datasheet: *Plotting graphs*.

(a) $y = x$ (b) $y = x^2$

(c) $y = x^3$ (d) $y = x^4$

(e) $y = \sqrt{x}$ (f) $y = \sqrt[3]{x}$

(g) $y = \dfrac{1}{x}$ (h) $y = \dfrac{1}{x^2}$

(i) $y = \sin x$ (j) $y = \cos x$

(k) $y = \tan x$ (l) $y = \log x$

(m) $y = 3^x$ (n) $y = \left(\dfrac{1}{2}\right)^x$

(o) $y = |x|$ (p) $y = \text{int}\,(x)$

2 Comment on the symmetry of graphs (a), (b), (c) and (d) in question 1.

3 Plot the graphs of $y = -x$, $y = -x^2$, $y = -x^3$ and $y = -x^4$.
How are they related to the graphs of question 2?

(Note: $-x^2$ means square first, then change sign. This can cause confusion sometimes with a graph plotter, and it may be necessary to include brackets, $-(x^2)$, to ensure the correct meaning.)

4 Compare the graphs of $y = x^2$ and $y = \sqrt{x}$.

The equation of a straight line

1 (a) Use a graph plotter to sketch the graph of $y = 2x + c$ where $c = -2, -1, 0, 1, 2$.

    (b) Describe the effect of varying c.

2 (a) Use a graph plotter to sketch the graph of $y = mx + 3$ where $m = -2, -1, 0, 1, 2$.

    (b) Describe the effect of varying m.

A gradient of 1 in 5, i.e. a rise of 1 unit for every 5 horizontal units travelled, is described mathematically as a gradient of $\frac{1}{5}$ or 0.2.

The gradient of a line measures how steeply it rises. Gradient is measured as

$$\frac{\text{vertical increase}}{\text{horizontal increase}}$$

Notice that if y decreases, then the 'vertical increase' will be negative.

E X A M P L E

Find the gradient of the line AB.

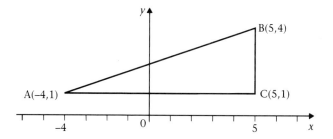

S O L U T I O N

The gradient is $\dfrac{\text{BC}}{\text{AC}} = \dfrac{3}{9} = \dfrac{1}{3}$

3 Plot the points A (1, 2) and B (3, 10) and calculate the gradient of the line AB.

4 Find the gradient of the line AB for

(a) A (−1, 2) B (2, 11)

(b) A (3, 1), B (−1, 9)

(c) A (4, 1), B (1, 1)

5

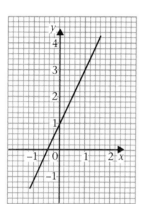

(a) Find the gradient of the line.

(b) Where does the line cross the y-axis?

(c) The equation of the line is $y = 2x + 1$. Show that the points (0, 1) and (2, 5) satisfy this equation.

(d) How can you relate the equation $y = 2x + 1$ to your answers to (a) and (b)?

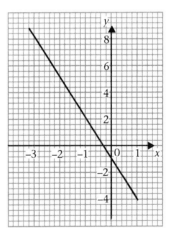

6 (a) Find the gradient of the line.

(b) Where does the line cross the y-axis?

(c) The equation of the line is $y = -3x - 1$. Choose two points, and show that their coordinates satisfy this equation.

(d) How can you relate the equation $y = -3x - 1$ to your answers to (a) and (b)?

7 Find the equation of the lines.

(a) (b)

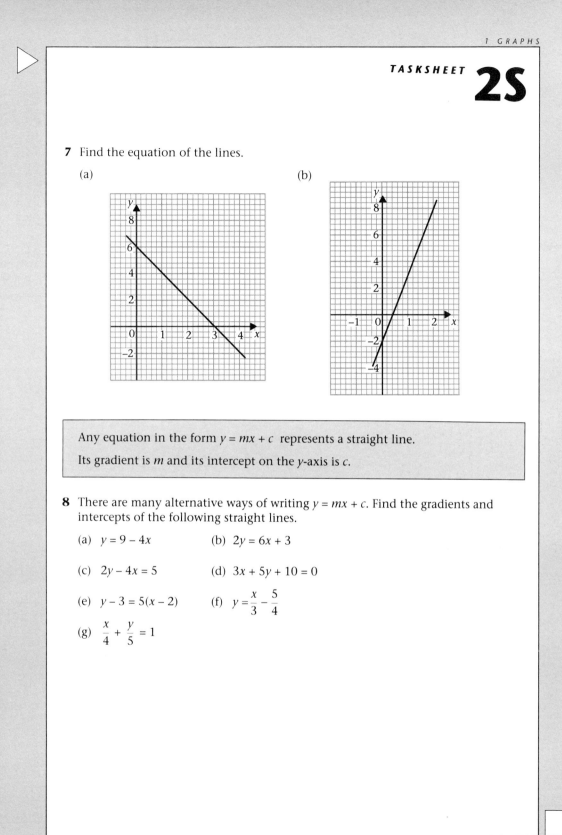

> Any equation in the form $y = mx + c$ represents a straight line.
>
> Its gradient is m and its intercept on the y-axis is c.

8 There are many alternative ways of writing $y = mx + c$. Find the gradients and intercepts of the following straight lines.

(a) $y = 9 - 4x$

(b) $2y = 6x + 3$

(c) $2y - 4x = 5$

(d) $3x + 5y + 10 = 0$

(e) $y - 3 = 5(x - 2)$

(f) $y = \dfrac{x}{3} - \dfrac{5}{4}$

(g) $\dfrac{x}{4} + \dfrac{y}{5} = 1$

Translations of the quadratic curve

1 Plot the graph of $y = x^2$ and superimpose the graph of $y = x^2 + 3$.

2 Superimpose various graphs of the form $y = x^2 + q$, for both positive and negative values of q. Write down your conclusions.

3 Plot the graph of $y = x^2$ and superimpose the graph of $y = (x + 4)^2$. Describe carefully the relationship between the graphs.

4 Repeat question 2 for the family of curves with equations $y = (x + p)^2$.

5 (a) Describe carefully how any curve of the form $y = (x + p)^2 + q$ is related to the curve $y = x^2$.

   (b) What are the coordinates of the vertex of the parabola $y = (x + p)^2 + q$?

   (c) What is the equation of its line of symmetry?

6 Suggest *possible* equations for the following curves. The curve $y = x^2$ is shown dotted in each case and the coordinates of the vertex are given. Use a graph plotter to check your equations.

(a)   (b)   (c)

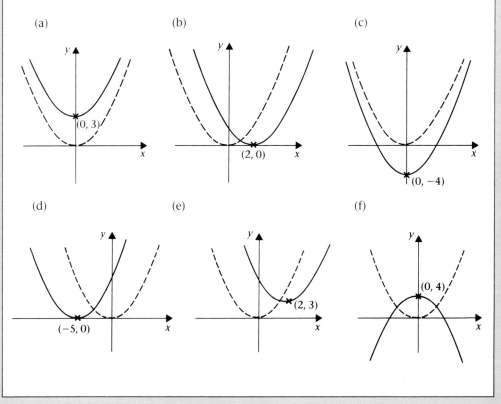

(d)   (e)   (f)

6 (Continued)

(g)   (h)   (i)

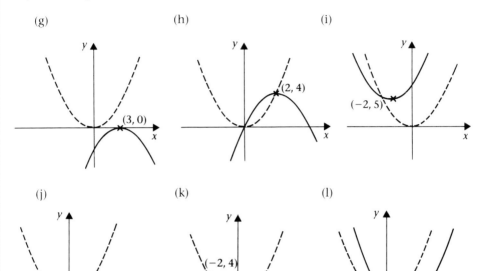

(j)   (k)   (l)

In this tasksheet you have found that the graph of $y = (x + p)^2 + q$ is a **translation** of the graph of $y = x^2$.

Using **vector notation**, this translation can be described as $\begin{bmatrix} -p \\ q \end{bmatrix}$
i.e. the curve is moved by $-p$ units in the x direction and by q units in the y direction.

This is an important result which will be used later.

Translations of the quadratic curve

1 By plotting various curves of the family $y = (x + p)^2 + q$ answer the following questions:

(a) How is the curve $y = (x + p)^2 + q$ related to $y = x^2$?

(b) What are the coordinates of its vertex?

(c) What is the equation of its line of symmetry?

(d) How do the values of p and q determine how many times the graph crosses the axes?

2 Suggest *possible* equations for the following curves. $y = x^2$ is shown dotted in each case and the coordinates of the vertex are given. Use a graph plotter to check your equations.

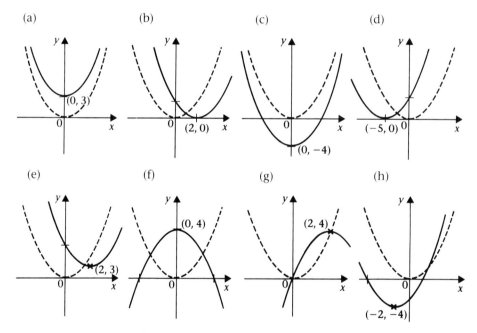

(a)   (b)   (c)   (d)

(e)   (f)   (g)   (h)

3 Sketch the curves $y = x^2 - 4$ and $y = 4 - x^2$. What are the coordinates of the points where they meet?

4 Sketch the curves $y = (x - 3)^2 + 2$ and $y = 11$ and find the coordinates of the points where they meet.

5 The curve $y = ax^2$ passes through the vertex of $y = (x + 2)^2 + 3$. What is the value of a?

6 The curves $y = (x - a)^2 + b$ and $y = (x - c)^2 + d$ never intersect. By comparing their graphs, find what relationships exist between any or all of a, b, c and d.

Multiplying brackets

You have met expressions like $3(x + 2)$ before.

$3(x + 2)$ means '3 lots of $(x + 2)$' or '3 lots of x' plus '3 lots of 2'.

i.e. $3(x + 2) = 3x + 6$.

1 Multiply out

(a) $5(x + 3)$ (b) $2(x - 4)$ (c) $8(2x + 5)$

(d) $-2(x + 6)$ (e) $-4(x - 7)$ (f) $6(x - 2y)$

Complicated expressions can sometimes be simplified by multiplication of any brackets, for example:

$$6x(x - 1) - 2\,(2x - 3) = 6x^2 - 6x - 4x + 6$$
$$= 6x^2 - 10x + 6$$

2 Multiply out and gather together like terms for

(a) $3 + 2(x + 3)$ (b) $3(x - 4)$ (c) $a + 5(8 - a)$

(d) $t - 4(1 - t)$ (e) $p - 1 + 2(3p - 8)$ (f) $5 - 6(5x - 9)$

(g) $y - 9(y - 2)$ (h) $4x - x(2 - x)$ (i) $2 - 3x(1 + 2x)$

You have seen how to multiply out expressions of the form $2x(x + 1)$. You can now consider expressions like $(x + 2)\,(x + 4)$.

$(x + 2)(x + 4)$ means 'x lots of $(x + 4)$' *plus* '2 lots of $(x + 4)$'.

So: $(x + 2)(x + 4)$ becomes $x(x + 4) + 2(x + 4)$
and the problem has been reduced to the earlier form with which you are familiar.

3 Multiply out

(a) $(x + 2)(x + 4)$ (b) $(x - 3)(x + 1)$

(c) $(x + 4)(x - 1)$ (d) $(x - 5)(x - 2)$

(e) $(x + 5)(x - 7)$ (f) $(x + 8)(x + 2)$

(g) $(x - 2)(x - 9)$ (h) $(x - 4)(x + 7)$

Expressions of the form $(x + 2)^2$ are called **perfect squares**. $(x + 2)^2$ means $(x + 2)(x + 2)$ and can be multiplied out in the standard way.

4 (a) Multiply out

(i) $(x + 3)^2$ (ii) $(x + 7)^2$ (iii) $(x - 9)^2$ (iv) $(x - 6)^2$

(b) If $(x + p)^2 = x^2 + bx + c$, express

(i) b in terms of p (ii) c in terms of p

Completing the square

You have seen that $(x + p)^2 + q$ is an alternative form of $x^2 + bx + c$ and that when written in this way it is easy to locate the vertex and sketch the quadratic. In this tasksheet you will learn how to express $x^2 + bx + c$ in the form $(x + p)^2 + q$. This is known as the **completed square form**.

1 (a) Plot the graph of $y = x^2$ and superimpose the graph of $y = x^2 + 2x$.

    (b) Consider the vertices to decide what translation maps $y = x^2$ onto $y = x^2 + 2x$. Hence write $x^2 + 2x$ in the form $(x + p)^2 + q$.

2 Taking values of b as (a) 10   (b) -6 (c) 7

    (i) plot the graph of $y = x^2$ and superimpose the graph of $y = x^2 + bx$;

    (ii) write down the translation which maps $y = x^2$ onto $y = x^2 + bx$. Hence write $x^2 + bx$ in the form $(x + p)^2 + q$.

3 (a) On the basis of your work in question 2 write $x^2 + 4x$ in the form $(x + p)^2 + q$.

    (b) Hence write $x^2 + 4x + 9$ in the form $(x + p)^2 + q$.

    (c) Check your answer to part (b) by plotting the graphs of $x^2 + 4x + 9$ and $(x + p)^2 + q$.

4 Write the following in the form $(x + p)^2 + q$.

    (a) $x^2 + 14x + 2$

    (b) $x^2 - 8x + 5$

    (c) $x^2 - 3x + 1$

    Use a graph plotter to check your answers.

5 (a) If $x^2 + bx = (x + p)^2 + q$, express p and q in terms of b.

    (b) Describe how you would express $x^2 + bx + c$ in completed square form.

Completing the square (algebraic approach)

5E

You have seen that $(x + p)^2 + q$ is an alternative form of $x^2 + bx + c$ and that when written in this way it is easy to locate the vertex and sketch the quadratic. In this tasksheet you will learn how to express $x^2 + bx + c$ in the form $(x + p)^2 + q$. This is known as the **completed square form**.

1 (a) Expand   (i) $(x + 5)^2$

                 (ii) $(x - 3)^2$

  (b) Express in the form $(x + p)^2$ (i) $x^2 + 4x + 4$

                                 (ii) $x^2 + 12x + 36$

                                (iii) $x^2 - 10x + 25$

  (c) If $x^2 + bx + c = (x + p)^2$, express   (i) p in terms of b

                                  (ii) c in terms of b

2 (a) Express $x^2 + 6x + 9$ in the form $(x + p)^2$.

  (b) Hence express $x^2 + 6x$ in the form $(x + p)^2 + q$.

  (c) Hence express $x^2 + 6x + 5$ in the form $(x + p)^2 + q$.

  (d) Sketch the graph of $y = x^2 + 6x + 5$.

3 (a) Express in the form $(x + p)^2 + q$ (i) $x^2 + 12x$

                                 (ii) $x^2 - 14x$

  (b) Hence write in completed square form   (i) $x^2 + 12x + 20$

                                   (ii) $x^2 - 14x + 80$

Although not all quadratics are perfect squares it is always possible to express them in the form $(x + p)^2 + q$ using the method developed above.

EXAMPLE

Express $x^2 - 8x + 3$ in the form $(x + p)^2 + q$.

SOLUTION

$x^2 - 8x = (x - 4)^2 - 16$ Find the square which fits the first two terms.

$\Rightarrow x^2 - 8x + 3 = (x - 4)^2 - 16 + 3$ Adjust your answer to take into account the constant term.

$\Rightarrow x^2 - 8x + 3 = (x - 4)^2 - 13$ With practice you may be able to obtain this line immediately.

4 Write these in the form $(x + p)^2 + q$.

(a) $x^2 + 14x + 2$

(b) $x^2 - 3x + 1$

(c) $x^2 + 8x - 3$

5 (a) Express $x^2 - 2x + 1$ in completed square form.

(b) Explain why $x^2 - 2x + 1$ can never be negative.

6 (a) Express $x^2 + bx + c$ in completed square form.

(b) Write down the coordinates of the vertex of the graph of $y = x^2 + bx + c$.

(c) What is the relationship that must be satisfied by b and c if the expression $x^2 + bx + c$ is always positive?

Factorised quadratics

1 (a) Plot the graph of $y = (x + 1)(x + 5)$. What is the significance of the numbers 1 and 5 with respect to the graph?

   (b) Investigate the graph of $y = (x + \alpha)(x + \beta)$ for various values of α and β, including positive and negative values, zero and the case where $\alpha = \beta$.

   (c) What is the significance of α and β for the graph?

2 What is the relationship between the graphs of

$$y = (x + \alpha)(x + \beta)$$

and

$$y = -(x + \alpha)(x + \beta)?$$

The quadratic expressions above are in **factorised form**.

3 Suggest possible equations for the following curves and use a graph plotter to check your answers.

(a) (b) (c)

3 (Continued)

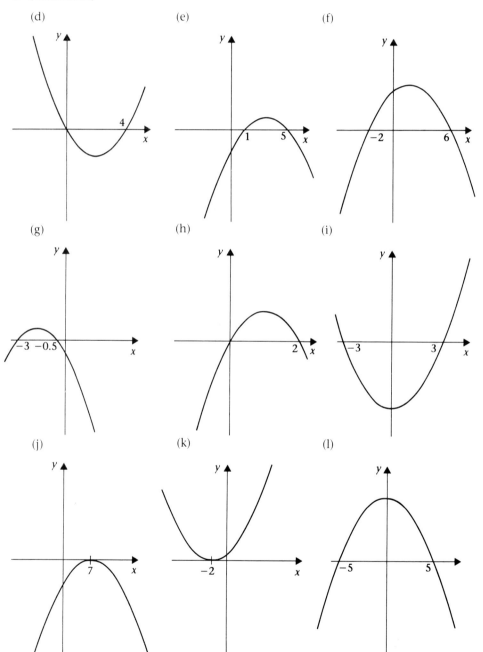

(d)

(e)

(f)

(g)

(h)

(i)

(j)

(k)

(l)

Further factorisation

7S

1 (a) Write in the form $x^2 + bx + c$.   (i) $(x + 2)(x + 3)$ (ii) $(x - 2)(x - 3)$

(iii) $(x + 4)(x + 5)$ (iv) $(x - 4)(x - 5)$

(b) How is the constant term c related to the numbers in the brackets?

(c) How is the coefficient b related to the numbers in the brackets?

When you multiply the brackets $(x + 4)(x + 7)$, you find

the coefficient of x by *adding* 4 to 7,

the constant term by *multiplying* 4 by 7.

$(x + 4)(x + 7) = x^2 + (4 + 7)x + 4 \times 7$

$\qquad\qquad\quad = x^2 + 11x + 28$

When you factorise $x^2 + 11x + 28$ you have to do the opposite and find two numbers

(a) whose product is +28 and (b) whose sum is +11.

Since 28 has a limited set of factors, i.e. $(\pm 28, \pm 1)$, $(\pm 14, \pm 2)$, $(\pm 7, \pm 4)$, it is not hard to see that the numbers must be 7 and 4.

2 Factorise

(a) $x^2 + 9x + 14$ (b) $x^2 + 13x + 40$ (c) $x^2 - 9x + 14$

(d) $x^2 + 12x + 36$ (e) $x^2 - 7x - 8$ (f) $x^2 + 3x - 28$

(g) $x^2 - 8x + 12$ (h) $x^2 - 5x - 36$ (i) $x^2 - 2x - 48$

(j) $x^2 + 2x - 24$

You should be familiar with the following important special cases:

- If the constant term is missing, x will be a factor, for example

  $x^2 + 6x = x(x + 6)$.

- If the expression has the form $x^2 - a^2$, then it factorises into $(x - a)\ (x + a)$, for example

  $x^2 - 16 = x^2 - 4^2 = (x - 4)\ (x + 4)$.

- Expressions of the form $x^2 + a^2$ will not factorise.

3 Factorise where possible

(a) $x^2 + 2x$ (b) $x^2 - 9$ (c) $x^2 - 8x$

(d) $x^2 + 25$ (e) $x^2 + 25x$ (f) $x^2 - 25$

(g) $x^2 + 1$ (h) $x^2 - 1$ (i) $x^2 - x$

2 Sequences

2.1 Sequences in action

Sequences, or lists of numbers, occur in many contexts. From an early age we learn simple sequences such as the 5-times table:

5, 10, 15, 20, 25, 30, . . .

or we look for patterns in puzzles such as

2, 1, 4, 2, 6, 3, 8, 4, . . .

Many sequences of figures occur in statistical data and are displayed using graphs and charts. In some cases the sequence is not totally predictable, yet it shows a pattern as in the graph showing the growth of CD sales in the late 1980s. In other cases, such as the fluctuations in the mortgage rate, there does not appear to be a pattern.

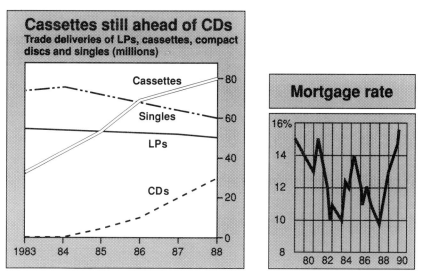

Sequences can also be used to predict future behaviour. In 1989 the population of Brazil was 160 million and was growing at 2.4 per cent per year. At this rate the population (in millions) over the next five years would be

163.84, 167.77, 171.80, 175.92, 180.14

What would be a sensible prediction for the population in 1995?

2.2 Generating sequences

To aid the description of a sequence, certain notations are used. If U is the sequence 3, 7, 11, 15, 19, . . . then

$u_1 = 3$ is the first term,

$u_2 = 7$ is the second term,

$u_5 = 19$ is the fifth term, etc.

(The dots at the end of the sequence indicate that further values exist.)

1 U is the sequence 2, 8, 14, 20, . . .

   (a) What are the values of u_1 and u_4?

   (b) What value would you expect for u_5?
        Give an equation connecting u_5 and u_4.

   (c) Give an equation connecting u_{i+1} and u_i.

2 T is the sequence defined by $t_1 = 4$ and $t_{i+1} = t_i + 9$.

   (a) What are the values of t_2, t_3, t_4, t_5?

   (b) What is the value of t_{20}?

A sequence U may be given by an **inductive definition**. Such a definition requires:

(i) a starting value or values, for example u_1, the first term;

(ii) a **recurrence relation**, i.e. a formula which will generate any term from the previous term or terms, for example $u_{i+1} = u_i + 6$.

TASKSHEET 1 – Patterns and sequences (page 48)

On tasksheet 1 you have seen sequences which illustrate a number of properties. All sequences can be classified as either **convergent** or **divergent.**

Convergent

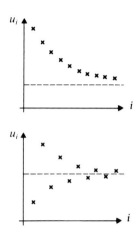

The values get closer and closer to a fixed value.

The values of this convergent sequence **oscillate** back and forth about one value.

Divergent

Any sequence which does not converge to a fixed value is called divergent.

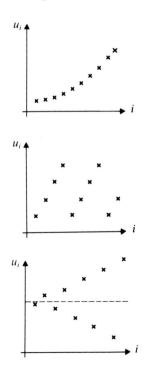

This sequence diverges to $+\infty$. The values grow in size, eventually becoming infinitely large.

This sequence is **periodic**. A set of values is repeated at regular intervals.

This sequence is both oscillatory and divergent.

EXAMPLE 1

Find an inductive definition for the series 1, 2, 6, 24, 120, . . .

SOLUTION

$u_1 = 1$ and the pattern is then: $u_2 = 2 \times u_1$, $u_3 = 3 \times u_2$, $u_4 = 4 \times u_3$, etc.

So $u_1 = 1$, $u_{i+1} = (i + 1)u_i$.

EXERCISE 1

1 Write down the first five terms of sequence U where $u_{i+1} = 2u_i$ and $u_1 = 4$ and describe the properties of the sequence.

2 Which of the following sequences converge?

   (a) $u_{i+1} = \dfrac{2}{3} u_i$, $u_1 = 9$ (b) $u_{i+1} = \dfrac{1}{u_i^2}$, $u_1 = 2$

   (c) $u_{i+1} = \dfrac{5}{u_i}$, $u_1 = 1$

3

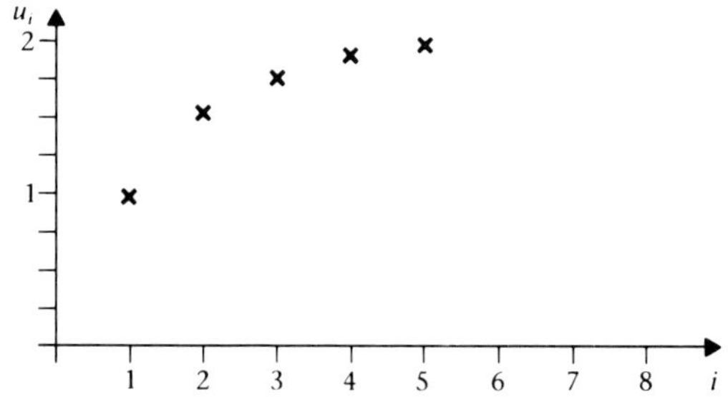

   The diagram above illustrates the first five terms of the sequence U where

   $$u_{i+1} = u_i + \left(\frac{1}{2}\right)^i \text{ and } u_1 = 1.$$

   Describe fully the properties of the sequence.

4 Investigate and describe the sequence T where $t_{i+2} = t_i + t_{i+1}$ and $t_1 = 1$, $t_2 = 2$.

5 Investigate and describe the sequence T where

   $$t_{i+1} = \frac{27}{(t_i)^2} \text{ and } t_1 = 2.$$

6 Find inductive definitions for the series:

   (a) $1, \dfrac{1}{2}, \dfrac{1}{4}, \dfrac{1}{8}, \dfrac{1}{16}, \ldots$ (b) $1, -\dfrac{1}{2}, \dfrac{1}{4}, -\dfrac{1}{8}, \dfrac{1}{16}, \ldots$

2.3 The general term

During a training run, a coach makes an athlete run at $6\,\mathrm{m\,s^{-1}}$. Let s_t metres be the distance covered in t seconds, so that $s_1 = 6$.

(a) What is s_{50}?   (b) What is s_t?

(c) Why is it inappropriate to use an inductive method to calculate s_{50}?

Clearly, there are drawbacks if only inductive definitions are used to generate the terms of a sequence. It can be very useful to have a formula for the general term.

(a) Why is $2 \times 3^{n-1}$ the general term of the sequence T where

$$t_{i+1} = 3t_i \text{ and } t_i = 2?$$

(b) What are the terms of the sequence U where

$$u_i = (-1)^i \frac{1}{i^2} ?$$

T A S K S H E E T 2 — The general term (page 50)

E X A M P L E 2

Find an expression for the ith term of the sequence $-1, 3, -5, 7, \ldots$

S O L U T I O N

It is helpful to think of the terms as

$$-1 \times 1, \quad +1 \times 3, \quad -1 \times 5, \quad +1 \times 7, \ldots$$

The $-1, +1, -1, +1, \ldots$ sequence is generated by $(-1)^i$.
The $1, 3, 5, 7, \ldots$ sequence is generated by $2i - 1$.
So $u_i = (-1)^i (2i - 1)$.

2.4 Arithmetic series

A car is accelerating from rest.

In the first second it moves 3 m.

In the second second it moves 5 m.

In the third second it moves 7 m.

In the fourth second it moves 9 m.

If this pattern continues, then the total distance travelled in the first ten seconds will be

$$S = 3 + 5 + 7 + 9 + 11 + 13 + 15 + 17 + 19 + 21.$$

A sequence of numbers added together is called a **series**. In this case S will be the sum of the series. To calculate S for the first ten seconds is straightforward, if a little tedious, but had the sum been for the first thirty seconds, an algebraic technique would have been useful.

> As a schoolboy, the German mathematician Gauss (1777–1855) spotted a simple fact which helped him to calculate the sum of the series
>
> $$1 + 2 + 3 + 4 + \ldots + 99 + 100.$$
>
> Can you find a simple way to sum this series?

Where consecutive terms of a sequence differ by a constant value, such a sequence is known as an **arithmetic sequence**, or **arithmetic progression (A.P.)**.

Gauss's observation makes it straightforward to sum any such series.

T A S K S H E E T   3   –   Arithmetic series (page 52)

> The average term of an arithmetic progression can be found by averaging the first and last terms. The sum of an A.P. is found by multiplying
>
> $$\text{number of terms} \times \text{average term}$$
>
> For a series of n terms with first term a and last term l, this can be written as
>
> $$S_n = \left(\frac{a + l}{2} \right) n$$
>
> or, if the common difference d is given instead of the last term,
>
> $$S_n = \frac{n}{2} \left\{ 2a + (n - 1)d \right\}$$

EXAMPLE 3

Sum the series   (a) $3 + 5 + 7 + \ldots + 99$

(b) $4 + 11 + 18 + \ldots$ as far as the 50th term

SOLUTION

(a) The first term is 3, the last 99, so the average is $(3 + 99)/2 = 51$.
The difference between the first and last terms is $99 - 3 = 96$.
With a common difference of 2, 99 is $\frac{96}{2} = 48$ terms on from 3.
Thus the total number of terms is $48 + 1 = 49$
and the sum is $49 \times 51 = 2499$.

(b) The first term $a = 4$, and the common difference $d = 7$, so from
the formula, $S_{50} = 25(8 + 49 \times 7) = 8775$.

EXERCISE 2

1   Find the sum of the arithmetic series

(a) $4 + 9 + 14 + 19 + \ldots + 199$

(b) $3 + 9 + 15 + \ldots$ as far as the 50th term

(c) $1 + 1\frac{1}{2} + 2 + 2\frac{1}{2} + \ldots + 100$

(d) $99 + 97 + 95 + \ldots + 25$

2   Complete the following table.

	First term	Common difference	Number of terms	Last term	Sum
(a)	8	2	18		
(b)	6	9		303	
(c)	3		25	195	

3   A small terrace at a football
ground comprises a series of 15
steps, which are 50 m long and
built of solid concrete. Each
step has a rise of $\frac{1}{4}$ m and a
tread of $\frac{3}{4}$ m.

By calculating the area under
each step and forming a series,
calculate the total volume of
concrete required to build the
terrace.

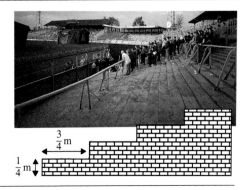

2.5 Finance

Jo has £1000 to invest. One building society offers her a rate of interest of 8 per cent per annum, whilst another offers a rate of 4 per cent payable every six months.

 Which scheme should Jo choose?

Now suppose that Jo wishes to save over a period of years. Every January for ten years, Jo invests her annual savings of £1000 and is paid at an annual rate of interest of 8 per cent.

> If Jo's savings at the start of year k are £S_k explain why her savings a year later, £S_{k+1}, are given by $S_{k+1} = S_k \times 1.08 + 1000$.

In practice, people save money and repay loans using various time intervals. A useful means of comparing different **notional rates** is known as the **APR** or **annual percentage rate**. This is described and explained in the case studies on tasksheet 4.

Mortgage schemes are particularly common as ways of financing the purchase of houses. A typical process is outlined in tasksheet 5.

TASKSHEETS 4 – Annual percentage rate (page 55)
AND 5   and Mortgages (page 58)

2.6 Sigma notation

In section 2.5, you saw that when Jo invests £1000 per year into a savings account which pays 8 per cent interest, her savings after k years, S_k, and $k + 1$ years, S_{k+1}, are related by

$$S_{k+1} = S_k \times 1.08 + 1000$$

This inductive definition is useful for programming a spreadsheet, but is less useful for generating a formula for her total savings.

You can think of Jo's savings over the ten year period as being a set of ten investments – the first gaining interest for the full ten years, the second gaining interest for nine years, etc.

> (a) How much is Jo's first investment of £1000 worth after ten years?
>
> (b) How much is Jo's second investment of £1000 worth at the end of the ten year period?
>
> (c) Explain why her total investment is worth
>
> $$£1000(1.08 + 1.08^2 + 1.08^3 + \ldots + 1.08^{10})$$
>
> after ten years.

Expressions such as £1000$(1.08 + 1.08^2 + 1.08^3 + \ldots + 1.08^{10})$ are cumbersome to handle and since each term is of the same form you can write it more easily using a shorthand notation, known as **sigma notation**. Sigma, written Σ, is a Greek letter, which to mathematicians means 'the sum of'. Using this notation you can write the above series as

$$S = \sum_{i=1}^{10} 1000\,(1.08^i) \quad \text{or} \quad 1000 \sum_{i=1}^{10} 1.08^i$$

> Why can the 1000 be taken outside the summation?

Stated fully, this reads:

S is the sum of the series obtained by successively substituting the values of $i = 1$ to $i = 10$ in the general term $1000\,(1.08^i)$.

EXAMPLE 4

Express the series $3 + 5 + 7 + 9 + \ldots + 99$ using Σ notation.

S O L U T I O N

The general term of the series is $2i + 3$.
The first term, 3, corresponds to $i = 0$ and the last, 99, corresponds to $i = 48$.

Thus the series is $\displaystyle\sum_{i=0}^{48} (2i + 3)$.

Is this the only way of expressing this series?

E X E R C I S E   3

1   Write out the terms of the following series.

(a) $\displaystyle\sum_{i=1}^{5} \frac{1}{i}$

(b) $\displaystyle\sum_{i=3}^{7} i^2$

(c) $\displaystyle\sum_{i=1}^{5} \frac{1}{i(i+1)}$

(d) $\displaystyle\sum_{i=4}^{8} (-1)^i (2i + 3)$

(e) $\displaystyle\sum_{i=0}^{5} (i+1)^3$

(f) $\displaystyle\sum_{i=1}^{6} i^3$

2   Rewrite using Σ notation.

(a) $\sqrt{1} + \sqrt{2} + \sqrt{3} + \ldots + \sqrt{50}$

(b) $2^2 + 4^2 + 6^2 + \ldots + 100^2$

(c) $\frac{1}{3} + \frac{1}{5} + \frac{1}{7} + \ldots + \frac{1}{99}$

(d) $1^3 - 2^3 + 3^3 - 4^3 + \ldots + 19^3$

(e) $\frac{1}{2} + \frac{2}{3} + \frac{3}{4} + \frac{4}{5} + \ldots + \frac{99}{100}$

3   Calculate the sum of the arithmetic series.

(a) $\displaystyle\sum_{i=1}^{20} (3i + 4)$

(b) $\displaystyle\sum_{i=5}^{24} (45 - 2i)$

T A S K S H E E T   6 E   –   *Using sigma (page 59)*

2.7 Geometric series

An arithmetic series is a special type of series whose pattern enables a simple formula to be developed.

The series which represented Jo's savings

$$£1000 \ (1.08 + 1.08^2 + 1.08^3 + \ldots + 1.08^{10})$$

can also be summed using a simple formula.

This series is an example of a **geometric progression (G.P.)** which is one in which each term increases by a constant multiple or **common ratio**, which in this case is 1.08.

Summing a geometric series is not as straightforward as summing an arithmetic series. To simplify matters ignore the 1000 and consider the sum of the series

$$S = 1.08 + 1.08^2 + 1.08^3 + \ldots + 1.08^{10} \qquad \textcircled{1}$$

The trick is to multiply by 1.08

$$1.08S = 1.08^2 + 1.08^3 + 1.08^4 + \ldots + 1.08^{11} \qquad \textcircled{2}$$

and then subtract the original series S.

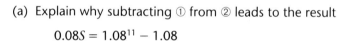

(a) Explain why subtracting ① from ② leads to the result

$$0.08S = 1.08^{11} - 1.08$$

(b) What is S, the amount Jo has saved after 10 years?

(c) Suggest other examples of G.Ps.

(d) Generalise the method for summing the G.P. to any G.P., where the first term is a and the common ratio is r.

In general, for the G.P. with first term a and common ratio r

$$a + ar + ar^2 + \ldots + ar^{n-1}$$

you can obtain the formula

$$\sum_{i=1}^{n} ar^{i-1} = a \ \frac{r^n - 1}{r - 1}$$

EXAMPLE 5

Find the sum of the series:

(a) $3 + 6 + 12 + \ldots + 3072$

(b) $\displaystyle\sum_{i=2}^{10} \left(\frac{1}{3}\right)^i$

SOLUTION

(a) The terms are $3, 3 \times 2, 3 \times 2^2, \ldots, 3 \times 2^{10}$.
The series is therefore a G.P. with first term 3, common ratio 2 and 11 terms.
Its sum is

$$3 \times \frac{2^{11} - 1}{2 - 1} = 6141$$

(b) The series is a G.P. with first term $\frac{1}{9}$, common ratio $\frac{1}{3}$ and 9 terms. Its sum is therefore

$$\frac{1}{9} \times \frac{(\frac{1}{3})^9 - 1}{(\frac{1}{3}) - 1} \approx 0.1667$$

EXERCISE 4

1 Calculate the sum of the series to the number of terms stated.

(a) $2 + 6 + 18 + 54 + \ldots$ (8 terms)

(b) $2 + 10 + 50 + 250 + \ldots$ (12 terms)

(c) $1 + 3 + 9 + 27 + \ldots$ (20 terms)

(d) $8 + 4 + 2 + 1 + \frac{1}{2} + \ldots$ (10 terms)

(e) $8 - 4 + 2 - 1 + \frac{1}{2} - \ldots$ (10 terms)

2 Calculate the sum of each series.

(a) $\displaystyle\sum_{i=1}^{5} 3^{i-1}$
(b) $\displaystyle\sum_{i=1}^{10} 8^{i-1}$
(c) $\displaystyle\sum_{i=1}^{7} 2^i$

(d) $\displaystyle\sum_{i=3}^{8} \left(\frac{1}{2}\right)^i$
(e) $\displaystyle\sum_{i=1}^{20} \left(-\frac{3}{4}\right)^{i-1}$

3 Legend tells that the Shah of Persia offered a reward to the citizen who introduced him to chess. The citizen asked merely for the number of grains of rice according to the rule:

1 grain for the first square on the chessboard,

2 grains for the second square,

4 grains for the third square,

8 grains for the fourth square and so on.

(a) How many grains of rice did he request?

(b) If a grain of rice weighs 0.02g, what weight of rice did he request?

4 Julius Caesar was born in 101 BC. If his mother had invested the Roman equivalent of 1p for him in a bank account which paid (a) 1 per cent; (b) 5 per cent interest per annum, how much would it have been worth in 1989?

5 The sum of £200 is invested annually at 5 per cent interest per annum. What is the total sum of money in the account at the end of 50 years?

6 Using a typical figure for a school leaver's salary and assuming that it will increase by 10 per cent annually, estimate a person's total earnings during their working life.

7 The sum of £1000 is invested annually at 7.5 per cent interest per annum.

(a) What is the total sum of money at the end of n years?

(b) How long will it take for the total sum of money to be twice the total amount invested?

TASKSHEET 7E – *Mortgages revisited (page 61)*

2.8 Infinity

So far, when you have summed series, you have taken a finite number of terms. Earlier, in section 2.2, you noticed that sequences show certain patterns of behaviour (for example convergence or divergence) as you take more and more terms. In the next tasksheet you will consider what happens to the sum as you take more and more terms in a series.

T A S K S H E E T   8   –   Zeno's paradox (page 62)

(a) Explain what is meant by a sum to infinity.

(b) In the previous section you found that

$$\sum_{i=1}^{n} ar^{i-1} = a\,\frac{r^n - 1}{r - 1}$$

(i) For what values of r will the series have a sum to infinity?

(ii) What is this sum?

An infinite G.P. can be summed providing the common ratio r satisfies $|r| < 1$.

$$a + ar + ar^2 + \ldots = \frac{a}{1 - r}, \text{ for } |r| < 1$$

E X A M P L E   6

Find the sum of the infinite series $1 + \dfrac{2}{3} + \dfrac{4}{9} + \dfrac{8}{27} + \ldots$

S O L U T I O N

First term $a = 1$

Common ratio $r = \dfrac{2}{3}$

$\Rightarrow$ Sum to infinity $S_\infty = \dfrac{1}{1 - \frac{2}{3}} = 3$

EXERCISE 5

1 Where possible, calculate the sum of the infinite series

(a) $\frac{9}{10} + \frac{9}{100} + \frac{9}{1000} + \ldots$

(b) $4 - 3 + \frac{9}{4} - \frac{27}{16} + \ldots$

(c) $1 - 2 + 4 - 8 + \ldots$

(d) $5 + \frac{5}{2} + \frac{5}{4} + \frac{5}{8} + \ldots$

2 Calculate the sum of

(a) $\displaystyle\sum_{i=1}^{\infty} \frac{1}{3^{i-1}}$

(b) $\displaystyle\sum_{i=1}^{\infty} (0.25)^{i-1}$

(c) $\displaystyle\sum_{i=1}^{\infty} 2^{-i}$

3 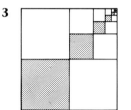 The diagram illustrates the infinite G.P.

$$\frac{1}{4} + \frac{1}{16} + \frac{1}{64} + \frac{1}{256} + \ldots$$

(a) Find the sum of the G.P.

(b) How could you see this result directly from the diagram?

4 Von Koch's 'snowflake' curve is shown below in its various stages of development. F_0 is an equilateral triangle; F_1 is derived from F_0 by trisecting each side and replacing the centre third of each side of the triangle by two sides of an equilateral triangle; F_2 is obtained in the same way from F_1 and so on.

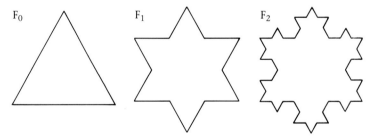

If each side of F_0 is of length 1 and P_n is the perimeter of the nth snowflake curve, write down

(a) P_0 (b) P_1 (c) P_2 (d) P_n.

What happens to the perimeter of the curve as $n \to \infty$?

5 How many terms of the series

$$2 + \frac{4}{5} + \frac{8}{25} + \frac{16}{125} + \ldots$$

must be taken before its sum to n terms differs from its sum to infinity by less than 0.01?

After working through this chapter you should:

1   know how to recognise, define and describe sequences;

2   be able to use Σ notation as a shorthand;

3   be able to define convergence to a limiting value;

4   be able to use the results:

  (i) arithmetic progression:

        sum = number of terms × average of first and last terms,

  (ii) geometric progression:

$$\sum_{i=1}^{n} ar^{i-1} = a \, \frac{1 - r^n}{1 - r} \text{ or } a \, \frac{r^n - 1}{r - 1};$$

$$\sum_{i=1}^{\infty} ar^{i-1} = \frac{a}{1 - r}, \quad \text{for } |r| < 1.$$

Patterns and sequences

Help is given in Technology datasheet: *Repeated calculations*.

1 For each sequence write out the first five terms and the value of the 20th term.

(a) $u_1 = -5$ and $u_{i+1} = u_i + 2$ (b) $u_1 = 15$ and $u_{i+1} = u_i - 4$

(c) $u_1 = 2$ and $u_{i+1} = 3u_i$ (d) $u_1 = 3$ and $u_{i+1} = \dfrac{1}{u_i}$

We can illustrate the behaviour of sequences using diagrams.

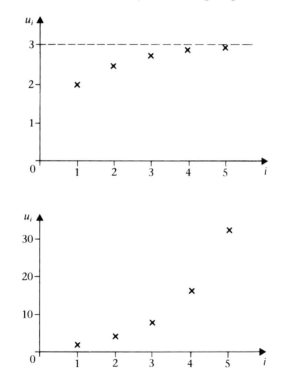

$2, 2\frac{1}{2}, 2\frac{3}{4}, 2\frac{7}{8}, 2\frac{15}{16}, \ldots$ converges; $2, 4, 8, 16, 32 \ldots$ diverges

2 For each of the sequences below, sketch a diagram to illustrate its behaviour (obtain sufficient terms to be able to describe the behaviour or pattern of the sequence). You may find it interesting to use a variety of starting values.

(a) $u_{i+1} = -2u_i$ (b) $u_{i+1} = 2u_i + 4$

(c) $u_{i+1} = (i+1)u_i$ (d) $u_{i+1} = \dfrac{1}{i+1}u_i$

(e) $u_{i+1} = \dfrac{2}{u_i}$ (f) $u_{i+1} = u_i + 2i + 1$

3 (a) For the sequence $u_{i+1} = \dfrac{1}{i+1} u_i$ and $u_1 = 1$, how many terms are needed before the answer becomes less than

   (i) $\dfrac{1}{1\,000\,000}$;   (ii) $\dfrac{1}{10^{10}}$?

   (b) For the sequence $u_{i+1} = (i+1)u_i$ and $u_1 = 1$, how many terms can be calculated before your calculator memory overflows?

   (N.B. $n \times (n-1) \times (n-2) \times \ldots \times 3 \times 2 \times 1$ is called **n factorial** and is written as $n!$ For example $5! = 5 \times 4 \times 3 \times 2 \times 1$. Most calculators have a facility to calculate these values.)

4E For different starting values, obtain a sufficient number of terms to enable you to describe the behaviour or patterns of each sequence.

   (a) $u_{i+2} = u_i + u_{i+1}$ (you will need starting values for both u_1 and u_2)

   (b) $u_{i+1} = \dfrac{20 - 3u_i}{2u_i}$ (you will need to generate a considerable number of terms to be sure of the pattern)

   (c) $u_{i+1} = 2u_i - 10 \, \text{INT} \left(\dfrac{u_i}{5} \right)$

5E Investigate the following sequence, using various whole number starting values.

$$s_i + 1 = \begin{cases} 3s_{i+1} & \text{when } s_i \text{ is odd} \\ \dfrac{s_i}{2}, & \text{when } s_i \text{ is even} \end{cases}$$

You are recommended to begin with starting values of between 1 and 10. What happens with numbers greater than 10?

The general term

TASKSHEET 2

1

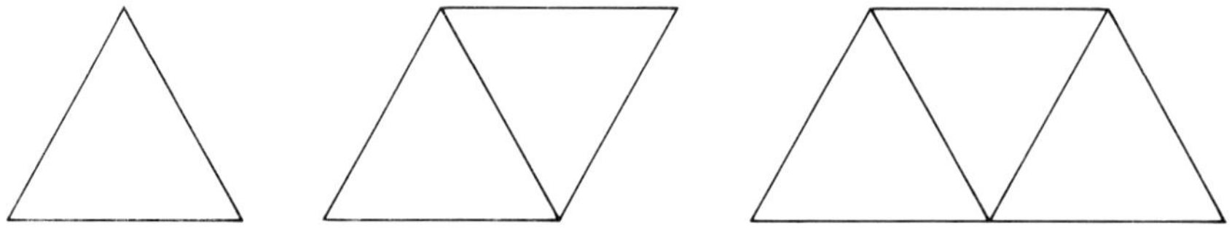

The set of patterns above can be made using matchsticks. How many matchsticks would be required for the next pattern in the sequence? Copy and complete the table.

No. of triangles	1	2	3	4	5	10	20	100	i
No. of matchsticks									

2 Copy and complete the table below for each of the following patterns of dots.

Position in pattern	1	2	3	4	5	10	20	100	i
No. of dots									

(a) 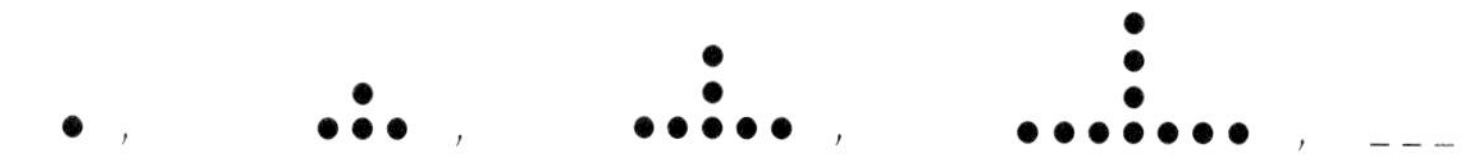

(b) 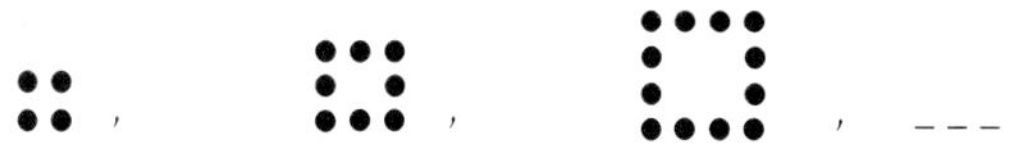

(c) 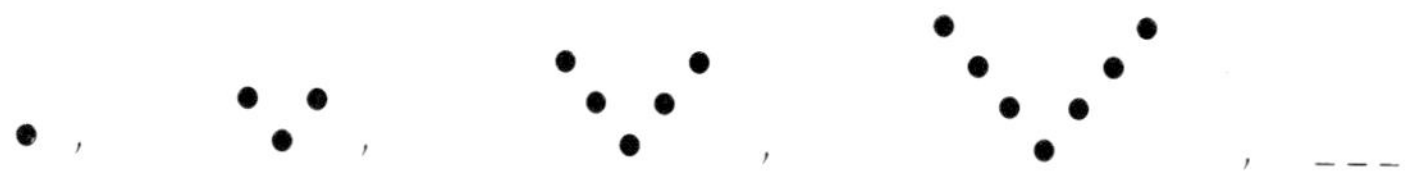

(d)

(e)

(f) 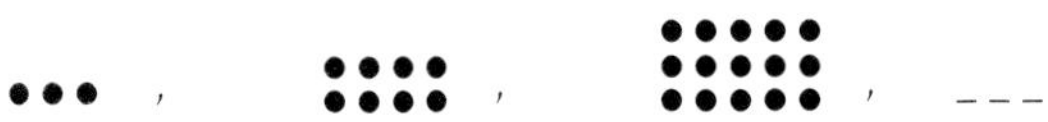

3 Write out the first 5 terms of the sequence whose ith term is

(a) $u_i = 3i + 2$

(b) $u_i = 5 \times 2^i$

(c) $u_i = 3i^2$

If a sequence comprises terms with alternating signs you can use a special technique to define the ith term. This is illustrated in the next question.

4 (a) Write out the first 5 terms of the sequence whose ith term is

   (i) $u_i = (-1)^i$

   (ii) $u_i = (-1)^{i+1}$

   (iii) $u_i = (-1)^{i+2}$

   (iv) $u_i = (-1)^i 2^{i-1}$

(b) Write down the general term of the sequence

   (i) 3, −3, 3, −3, 3, . . .

   (ii) −3, 3, −3, 3, −3, . . .

A sequence of alternating signs can be achieved by using a factor of $(-1)^i$ or $(-1)^{i+1}$ in the general term.

---

5 For each of the following sequences complete the table.

					Term					
	1	2	3	4	5	6	9	100	i	
A	2	4	6	8						
B	2	5	8	11						
C	2	4	8	16						
D	6	12	24	48						
E	1	−1	1	−1						
F	−1	2	−3	4						
G	1	−2	3	−4						
H	2	−4	6	−8						
I	$\frac{1}{2}$	$\frac{1}{3}$	$\frac{1}{4}$	$\frac{1}{5}$						
J	1	−4	9	−16						

Arithmetic series

$$1 + 2 + 3 + 4 + 5 + 6 + 7 + 8 + 9 + 10$$

This series may be summed by noting how each pair of values has the same sum. This was the property spotted by Gauss.

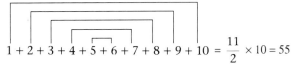

$$1 + 2 + 3 + 4 + 5 + 6 + 7 + 8 + 9 + 10 = \frac{11}{2} \times 10 = 55$$

You can use this method to find the sum of any arithmetic series.

1 (a) Find the sum of

(i) $1 + 2 + 3 + 4 + \ldots + 20$

(ii) $1 + 2 + 3 + 4 + \ldots + 9$ (careful!)

(iii) $1 + 2 + 3 + 4 + \ldots + 29$

(b) Describe in your own words how to sum an arithmetic series.

2 Show that the series

$$5 + 6 + 7 + \ldots + 105$$

has 101 terms.

3 For the series below, state the number of terms and sum the series.

(a) $1 + 2 + 3 + 4 + \ldots + 50$

(b) $10 + 11 + 12 + \ldots + 90$

(c) $200 + 199 + 198 + \ldots + 100$

For an arithmetic series, whose first term is a and last term l, the sum of the first n terms, S_n, is given by:

$$S_n = \left(\frac{a + l}{2} \right) n$$

---

4 For the series below, state the number of terms and use the result above to sum the series.

(a) $1 + 3 + 5 + 7 + 9 + 11 + 13 + 15$

(b) $4 + 7 + 10 + 13 + \ldots + 100$

(c) $196 + 191 + 186 + \ldots + 71$

For some series, instead of being given the last term, you are given the number of terms. If this is the case you need to find the last term.

5 For each of the series below, find a formula in terms of i for the ith term.

   (a) $3 + 5 + 7 + 9 + \ldots$

   (b) $6 + 10 + 14 + 18 + \ldots$

   (c) $12 + 7 + 2 - 3 - \ldots$

6 For the series $5 + 9 + 13 + 17 + \ldots$

   (a) (i)   calculate the 15th term;

        (ii) calculate the sum of the first 15 terms.

   (b) (i)   Write down an expression for the ith term;

        (ii) find a formula for the sum of the first i terms.

You can generalise the method of question 6 to a series having first term a and where each succeeding term is found by adding on d.

d is called the **common difference** for the sequence.

The first few terms are:

   $a, a + d, a + 2d, \ldots$

7 For the sequence $a, a + d, a + 2d, \ldots$, write down

   (a) the fifth term;

   (b) the 50th term;

   (c) the nth term;

   (d) the sum of the first 50 terms.

To obtain a general formula for the sum of n terms of the series, you need:

   the first term $= a$
   the last term $= a + (n - 1)d$

8 Show (by substitution into the earlier form for S_n) that the sum of n terms of the series is

$$S_n = n \, \frac{[2a + (n - 1)d]}{2} = \frac{n}{2} \, [2a + (n - 1)d]$$

> For an arithmetic series, whose first term is a and whose common difference is d, a useful formula for the sum of the first n terms is
>
> $$S_n = \frac{n}{2}\left[2a + (n-1)\,d\right]$$

9 Use the formula above to find the sum of

(a) $2 + 7 + 12 + 17 + \ldots$ as far as the 20th term

(b) $19 + 16 + 13 + 10 + \ldots$ as far as the 50th term

10 A child builds a pattern with square building bricks using the sequence of steps as shown:

The total number of bricks used is $1 + 3 + 5 + \ldots$

(a) How many bricks does the child use on the nth step?

(b) If the child has 60 bricks, how many steps can be completed?

(c) Use the formula for summing an arithmetic series to show that the total number of bricks used will be n^2.

11E Another child builds a square pattern using bricks that are twice as long as they are wide.

(a) How many bricks does the child use on the nth step?

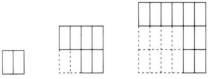

(b) Use the formula for summing an arithmetic series to find the total number of bricks used.

12E Each year Mrs Smith gives her nephew a birthday present of money (in £) equal to five times his age in years. The money is put into a bank account, but unfortunately does not attract any interest and he is not allowed to withdraw any money until he is 18. She makes the first payment on his first birthday and continues until he is 18.

(a) How much does he have in the account on his 18th birthday?

(b) How old is he when the sum of money in the account first exceeds £500?

13E 220 m of video tape are wound onto a reel of circumference 8.2 cm. Because of the thickness of the tape, each turn is 0.1 cm longer than the previous one. How many turns are required?

Annual percentage rate (APR)

When borrowing money or deciding where to put savings, the interest rate is not the only factor to be taken into account. When obtaining a house mortgage, for example, it can be very important that the building society or bank should be able to confirm the loan without a long waiting period. Similarly it might be necessary to accept a low interest rate on savings in order to be able to withdraw the money at short notice.

Nevertheless, it is important that anyone considering borrowing should be able to compare interest rates such as those above.

11 per cent per annum

The customer repays

$$£277.50 \times 12 = £3330$$

and so has paid £330 in interest charges. Since

$$£3000 \times \tfrac{11}{100} = £330$$

the stated rated of 11 per cent is easy to understand.

The 11 per cent is called a flat rate and, although it is easy to understand, it is nevertheless misleading. The customer certainly pays 11 per cent interest on the £3000 but does **not** have the use of the full £3000 for a full year!

1 A loan of £800 is repaid by 12 monthly instalments of £100. What is the flat rate of interest?

1.65 per cent per month

This rate is also easy to understand. The customer pays 1.65 per cent interest on the amount owed during the month.

After one month the customer owes the original £3000 and interest of £3000 × 0.016 5 = £49.50: a total of £3049.50. (A quick way of obtaining this total is to calculate £3000 × 1.016 5). Since the customer repays £277.50, the amount owing throughout the second month is £2772.

To find the amount owing after two months, the procedure is repeated. The outstanding debt after two months is (£2772 × 1.016 5) − £277.50 = £2540.24.

2 Use either a spreadsheet or a simple computer program to continue the procedure for 12 months.
Help is given on Technology datasheet: *Repeated calculations*.

The debt is repaid after 12 months. Surprisingly, the flat rate of 11 per cent per annum and the rate of 1.65 per cent per month are equivalent!

21.7 per cent APR

The concept of APR or **annual percentage rate** is used to give consumers a simple way of comparing various methods of borrowing. Finance houses are currently obliged by law to quote the equivalent APR.

The APR corresponding to the rate of 1.65 per cent per month can be found by calculating the total interest on a year's loan, **assuming the entire repayment is at the end of the year**.

Suppose £100 is borrowed. After one month the amount outstanding is

£100 × 1.016 5 = £101.65.

After two months, the amount has become

£101.65 × 1.016 5

and so on.

3 By finding the amount to be repaid after 12 months, show that the APR is 21.7 per cent.

Remarkably, the three rates of 21.7 per cent APR, 11 per cent per annum and 1.65 per cent per month are **all** equivalent! When considering ways of borrowing money, the APR enables sensible comparisons to be made.

Further questions

4 Find the APR corresponding to monthly payments based on interest rates per month of

(a) 1 per cent   (b) 2 per cent   (c) 5 per cent.

5 Describe an algorithm or procedure for converting any monthly interest rate into an APR.

6 By trial and error using the method you found in question 5, find the monthly interest rate that corresponds to an APR of 100 per cent.

7 Use a computer or programmable calculator to show the amounts outstanding in successive months for any inputs of the initial loan, monthly interest rate and monthly repayments.

8 A loan of £800 is repaid by 5 monthly instalments of £200. Use your solution to question 7 and any appropriate method to find the monthly interest rate. Hence find the APR.

9

12.4% APR

TYPICAL EXAMPLE BX 16RE FINANCED
BY A HIRE PURCHASE AGREEMENT

CASH PRICE (ON THE ROAD)	£ 7,292.86
DEPOSIT (30%)†	£ 2,187.86
BALANCE	£ 5,105.00
36 EQUAL MONTHLY PAYMENTS OF	£ 127.52*
1 TERMINAL RENTAL	£ 1,786.75
TOTAL PAYABLE	£ 8,565.33

*36 monthly payments of £127.52 is equivalent to approx £29.43 per week. † MINIMUM DEPOSIT 20%

The figures in this car advertisement are the result of certain calculations. The 'terminal rental' is a final cash payment to clear any remaining debt.

(a) Explain how the figure of £2187.86 was obtained.

(b) How is the figure of £8565.33 obtained from the other figures?

(c) Show that £29.43 per week and £127.52 per month are equivalent.

(d) Find the monthly interest rate corresponding to an APR of 12.4 per cent.

Mortgages

A mortgage is a way of borrowing money in order to purchase a house, which is then used as security for the loan. A mortgage is usually taken out with a building society or bank, although it is also possible to take out a mortgage with other institutions such as a county council.

In order to understand how the simplest kind of mortgage works, you can see what happens in the case of a mortgage of £40000 borrowed at an interest rate of 10 per cent (the current mortgage rate may be different from this). The repayments are commonly made for 20 or 25 years, although this can be varied. Suppose you make monthly repayments of £395. How many years will it take to repay the loan?

1 Complete the following:

£

YEAR ONE:	Initial loan	40000
	Interest	
	Total debt	___
	Repayments 12 @ £395	4740
	Outstanding balance	___

(interest for the year is added at the beginning of the year)

YEAR TWO: Loan outstanding	
Interest	
Total debt	___
Repayments 12 @ £395	
Outstanding balance	___

This continues until the loan is completely repaid.

2 If $£L_n$ is the loan outstanding at the beginning of year n,

(a) write down L_1;

(b) express L_{n+1} in terms of L_n.

3 Use a program to find how long it will take to repay the mortgage. Help is given on Technology datasheet: *Repeated calculations*.

Using sigma

In manipulating series, sigma notation can be a very powerful and useful notation. To exploit it to the full you need to become confident in its use.

1 For the series $u_1 + u_2 + u_3 + \ldots + u_n$

   (a) Write down an expression for the sum of the series in sigma notation.

   (b) Write down a simple series and investigate the effect on the sum of the series when each term of the series is multiplied by the same constant.

   (c) Show that $\displaystyle\sum_{i=1}^{n} au_i = a\left(\sum_{i=1}^{n} u_i\right)$ for any constant a.

2 (a) Investigate how the sum of a series changes when you add a constant to each term of the series.

   (b) Show that $\displaystyle\sum_{i=1}^{n} (u_i + b) = \left(\sum_{i=1}^{n} u_i\right) + nb$

   (c) Show that $\displaystyle\sum_{i=1}^{n} (au_i + b) = a\left(\sum_{i=1}^{n} u_i\right) + nb$

For any constants a and b,

$$\sum_{i=1}^{n} (au_i + b) = a\left(\sum_{i=1}^{n} u_i\right) + nb$$

E X A M P L E

Evaluate $\displaystyle\sum_{i=1}^{n} (4i + 2)$.

S O L U T I O N

$$\sum_{i=1}^{n} (4i + 2) = 4\left(\sum_{i=1}^{n} i\right) + 2n$$

$$\sum_{i=1}^{n} i = \frac{n(n + 1)}{2}, \text{ using the formula for the sum of an arithmetic series.}$$

So $\displaystyle\sum_{i=1}^{n} (4i + 2) = \frac{4n(n + 1)}{2} + 2n = 2n^2 + 4n$

3 Find (a) $\displaystyle\sum_{i=1}^{n} (2i - 3)$ (b) $\displaystyle\sum_{i=1}^{n} (5i + 1)$

4 Generalise the result of question 2 by showing that

$$\sum_{i=1}^{n} (u_i + v_i) = \left(\sum_{i=1}^{n} u_i \right) + \left(\sum_{i=1}^{n} v_i \right)$$

5 (a) Write down the result of subtracting $1^3 + 2^3 + \ldots + n^3$ from $2^3 + 3^3 + \ldots + (n + 1)^3$.

    (b) Hence show that

$$\sum_{i=1}^{n} (i + 1)^3 - \sum_{i=1}^{n} i^3 = (n + 1)^3 - 1$$

    (c) Simplify $(i + 1)^3 - i^3$ and show that

$$\sum_{i=1}^{n} (i + 1)^3 - \sum_{i=1}^{n} i^3 = 3 \sum_{i=1}^{n} i^2 + 3 \sum_{i=1}^{n} i + n$$

    (d) Hence obtain the formula

$$\sum_{i=1}^{n} i^2 = \frac{n}{6} (n + 1) (2n + 1)$$

6 Use the result you have obtained in question 5 to find the sum of the first 99 squares.

7 Use the method of question 4 and the result from question 5 to find

    (a) $\displaystyle\sum_{i=1}^{n} (2i^2 - 6i + 4)$ (b) $1^2 + 3^2 + 5^2 + 7^2 + \ldots + (2n - 1)^2$

You should now be familiar with the following results

$$1 + 2 + 3 + \ldots + n = \sum_{i=1}^{n} i = \frac{n}{2} (n + 1)$$

$$1^2 + 2^2 + 3^2 + \ldots + n^2 = \sum_{i=1}^{n} i^2 = \frac{n}{6} (n + 1) (2n + 1)$$

$$\sum_{i=1}^{n} (au_i + bv_i) = a \sum_{i=1}^{n} u_i + b \sum_{i=1}^{n} v_i$$

Mortgages revisited

It is possible to set up an algebraic calculation for the repetitive routine you used to solve the mortgage problem on tasksheet 5.

YEAR ONE: Final debt $= 40000 \times 1.1 - 4740$

YEAR TWO: Final debt $= (40000 \times 1.1 - 4740) \times 1.1 - 4740$

$\qquad\qquad\qquad\quad = 40000 \times 1.1^2 - 4740 \times 1.1 - 4740$

1 Obtain similar expressions for the final debts at the end of year three and year four.

After n years, the outstanding debt

$$= 40000 \times 1.1^n - 4740 \times 1.1^{n-1} - 4740 \times 1.1^{n-2} - \ldots$$
$$\qquad\qquad - 4740 \times 1.1^2 - 4740 \times 1.1 - 4740$$

$$= 40000 \times 1.1^n - 4740 \,(1.1^{n-1} + 1.1^{n-2} + \ldots + 1.1^2 + 1.1 + 1)$$

$$= 40000 \times 1.1^n - 4740 \sum_{i=1}^{n} 1.1^{i-1} \qquad ①$$

2 (a) Explain why

$$\sum_{i=1}^{n} 1.1^{i-1} = \frac{1.1^n - 1}{0.1}$$

(b) Hence simplify expression ① for the outstanding debt after n years.

3 Find the monthly repayment required so that a mortgage of £50000 at 11 per cent per annum is repaid at the end of 25 years.

Zeno's paradox

In a paradox, two different, seemingly sound arguments lead to contradictory conclusions. The Greek, Zeno of Elia (c.450 BC), expounded a famous set of paradoxes on the subject of motion. The following is an illustration of one of them.

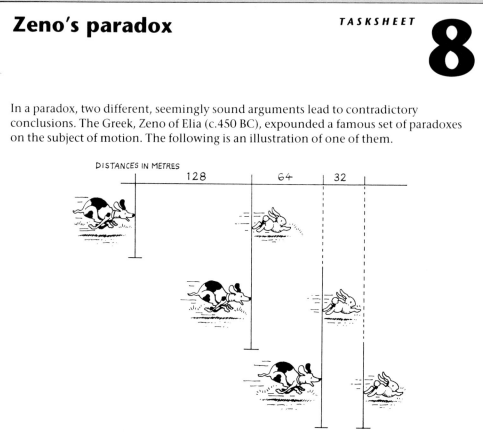

DISTANCES IN METRES

The dog chasing the rabbit is running at 8 m s⁻¹ and the rabbit at 4 m s⁻¹. Both are running in a straight line. When the dog first spotted the rabbit the distance between them was 128 m.

Now consider Zeno's argument.

1 (a) When the dog has run 128 m the rabbit will have moved away. How far will it have moved?

   (b) When the dog has run the next 64 m, the rabbit will have moved away again. How far will it have moved?

   (c) When the dog has run the next 32 m, the rabbit will have moved away again. How far will it have moved?

Each time the dog arrives at a position previously occupied by the rabbit it will have moved away. Thus the rabbit will always be in front of the dog and it will never be caught.

2 The distance in metres travelled by the dog in the first five intervals is

$$128 + 64 + 32 + 16 + 8$$

(a) Work out the sum for the first n intervals.

(b) What is the value of the sum for an infinite number of intervals?

3 The distance in metres travelled by the rabbit in the first five intervals is

$$64 + 32 + 16 + 8 + 4$$

(a) Work out the sum for the first n intervals.

(b) What is the value of the sum for an infinite number of intervals?

It appears to take an infinite number of steps for the dog to catch the rabbit.

4 (a) How far will the dog run in 40 seconds?

(b) How far will the rabbit run in 40 seconds?

(c) After 40 seconds, which animal will be in the lead?

5 From your answer to question 4 it is clear that the dog *will* catch the rabbit. Can you explain the fallacy in the arguments which led to the conclusions stated after questions 1 and 3?

Other entertaining paradoxes are outlined in the book *Riddles in Mathematics* by Eugene P. Northrop, Penguin.

3 Functions and graphs

3.1 Function notation

A scientist performs an experiment to investigate the absorption of light by a liquid. Light is shone through a coloured solution and the intensity of light emerging is measured.

She finds that if she varies the concentration of the solution her readings are as follows:

Concentration (mg cm^{-3})	c	0	0.2	0.4	0.6	0.8	1.0
Intensity (lux)	L	20.0	17.4	15.2	13.2	11.5	10.0

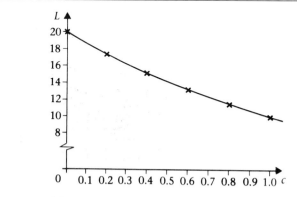

The two variables are related by the formula

$$L = \frac{20}{2^c}$$

This is known as Beer's law of absorption.

The formula can be used to calculate the value of L for any given value of c.

It is often helpful to consider an expression from a different point of view and consider it as a device which gives an **output** for any given **input**. In this case the input is c and the output is L.

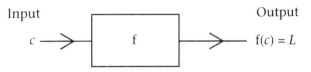

In other words, if the scientist inputs any value of c into her formula she will get a corresponding output which tells her the value of L. This dependence on c can be emphasised by use of the **function notation** $L = f(c)$, where the function f is given by

$$f(c) = \frac{20}{2^c}$$

This gives a convenient shorthand, since you can immediately write $f(0) = 20$, $f(1) = 10$ and so on.

Compare the notations

$$f(c) = \frac{20}{2^c} \text{ and } L = \frac{20}{2^c}$$

What are the advantages and disadvantages of each notation?

E X E R C I S E 1

1   If $f(x) = x^2 + 3$ for all values of x, find the values of

(a) f(0)   (b) f(1)   (c) f($\sqrt{2}$)   (d) f(–1)

2   If $g(t) = \dfrac{5}{3^t}$ for all values of t, find

(a) g(2)   (b) g(1)   (c) g(0)   (d) g(–1)   (e) g(x)

3   (a) If $f(x) = x^2 + 3x + 2$, find

(i) f(1)   (ii) f(−2)   (iii) f(0)   (iv) f(−1)   (v) f(n)

(b) If $f(y) = y^2 + 3y + 2$, find

(i) f(1)   (ii) f(−2)   (iii) f(0)   (iv) f(−1)   (v) f(n)

(c) Does f(x) differ from f(y)?

3.2 Using function notation

The graphs of $f(x) = x^2$ and $y = x^2 + 6x + 5$ are given below.

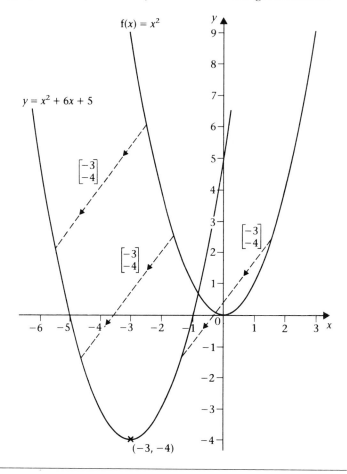

(a) Write down y in completed square form.

(b) What is $f(x + 3) - 4$?

TASKSHEET 1 — Translations (page 74)

Function notation gives a simple and easy way of describing a general property of functions and their associated graphs:

> Any function of the form $f(x + a) + b$ has a graph which is a translation by $\begin{bmatrix} -a \\ b \end{bmatrix}$ of the graph of $f(x)$.

3.3 Defining functions

You saw in section 3.1 that Beer's Law of Absorption can be stated as

$$f(c) = \frac{20}{2^c}$$

Why would it be meaningless to calculate $f(-2)$ or $f(1\,000\,000)$?

The precise **definition** of a function consists of two parts.

The **rule**:   this tells you how values of the function are assigned or calculated.

The **domain**:   this tells you the set of values to which the rule may be applied.

For example, $f(x) = \sqrt{x - 5}, x \geq 5$ defines a function f, where

the **rule** is $f(x) = \sqrt{x - 5}$

the **domain** is $x \geq 5$

In describing the domain of a function the following shorthand is useful for defining important sets:

$\mathbb{N}$ – the natural numbers 1, 2, 3, . . .

$\mathbb{Z}$ – the integers . . ., –3, –2, –1, 0, 1, 2, 3, . . .

$\mathbb{Q}$ – the rational numbers (or fractions)

$\mathbb{R}$ – the real numbers (both rational and irrational such as $\sqrt{2}$ and $-\pi$)

This notation can be extended using $^+$ and $^-$ signs. Thus $\mathbb{R}^+$ means the positive real numbers, $\mathbb{Z}^-$ means the negative integers.

You can also use the Greek letter $\in$ to mean 'belongs to'. Thus $x \in \mathbb{Q}^+$ means 'x belongs to the set of positive rationals'.

Use the new notation to define h, where

$$h(x) = \sqrt{x}, x \geq 0$$

When a function is written down, both the rule and the domain should be given. However, in practice the domain is often omitted and the function is assumed to be defined for all values that are valid in the rule. This is a common 'misuse' of the description of a function.

EXERCISE 2

1 If $f(x) = \dfrac{1}{x+2}$,

(a) find

(i) f(0)   (ii) f(−1)   (iii) f(a)   (iv) f(a − 2)   (v) f(−2)

(b) What is the largest possible domain for f?

(c) Sketch the graph of f(x).

2 If $h(x) = \sqrt{x}$, find the values of

(a) (i) h(2)   (ii) h(9)   (iii) h($\sqrt{2}$)   (iv) h(π)   (v) h(π²)

(b) What is the largest possible domain for h?

(c) Sketch the graph of h(x − 3).

3 Write down the largest possible domain for g in each of the following.

(a) $g(x) = \dfrac{1}{x+5}$ (b) $g(x) = \dfrac{1}{\sqrt{x-3}}$

(c) $g(x) = \sqrt[3]{x}$ (d) $g(x) = \dfrac{1}{\sqrt[3]{x+2}}$

4 The modulus function |x|, meaning 'the magnitude of x', is defined as

$$|x| = \begin{cases} x, & x \geq 0 \\ -x, & x < 0 \end{cases}$$

(On some calculators it is called abs(x), which is an abbreviation for 'the absolute value of x'.)

(a) Find the value of

(i) |5| (ii) |−7| (iii) $|\sqrt{2}|$ (iv) |−π| (v) |0|

(b) What is the largest possible domain for the function?

(c) Sketch the graph of

(i) y = |x|

(ii) y = |x − 2|

(iii) y = |x − 2| + 4

3.4 To plot or to sketch?

In the previous two sections you looked at many different functions. Now you will investigate the general properties and techniques used for obtaining the graphs of functions. You will be **sketching** graphs rather than **plotting** them. You can illustrate why sketching is often better than plotting if you use the plotting method to draw the graph of the function.

$$y = 4x + \frac{1}{2x - 5} \text{ for } x \in \mathbb{R}^+$$

This gives the table of values and plotted points as follows:

x	1	2	3	4	5
y	3.7	7.0	13.0	16.3	20.2

(a) What do you think the graph of $y = 4x + \dfrac{1}{2x - 5}$ looks like?

(b) What are the values of y when $x = 2.45, 2.49, 2.499$?

(c) What happens when $x = 2.5$?

(d) Use the graph plotter to draw the graph for values of x from 0 to 5.

Did you expect the graph to look like this?

You have seen that drawing a 'smooth curve' through selected points can lead to major errors. In general, for functions it helps to have an idea of what the graph will look like before you attempt the sketch.

> Sketching a curve implies having a good overall impression of its shape without the need for detailed plotting of points.

3.5 Features of graphs

To obtain the overall shape of a graph you only need to consider some of the major features.

T A S K S H E E T 2 – Dominance (page 75)

The tasksheet developed some of the ideas that can be used to build up an impression of a graph of a polynomial function.

> For a general polynomial function of the form
>
> $$y = ax^m + \ldots + bx^n + c \ (a, b \text{ are non-zero})$$
>
> where m is the highest power of x and n is the lowest non-zero power of x, the graph will look like $y = ax^m$ for very large x, look like $y = bx^n + c$ for very small x and will cross the y-axis at c.

E X A M P L E 1

Sketch the graph of $f(x) = 4x^3 - 6x^2 - 11x + 18$.

S O L U T I O N

(i) For large x the graph behaves like $y = 4x^3$.

(ii) For small x the graph behaves like $-11x + 18$.

Using just these features, you can draw part of the graph:

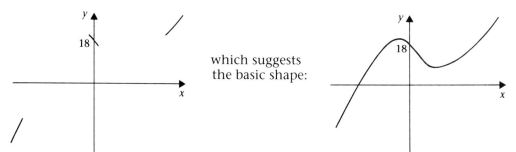

which suggests the basic shape:

The graph of example 1 might take any of the forms:

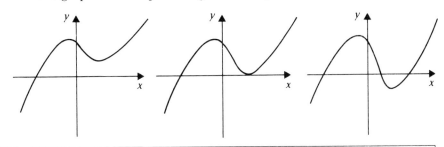

What further information do you need in order to establish which is the correct form?

When a polynomial function is given in factorised form, the roots give you extra clues to help determine the shape of the graph.

EXAMPLE 2

Sketch the graph of $f(x) = (x - 2)^2 (2x + 7)$.

SOLUTION

(i) $f(0) = 28$.

(ii) For large x, $2x^3$ is dominant.

(iii) The zeros of the function are at $x = 2$ and $x = -3\frac{1}{2}$.

The available information is plotted as shown:

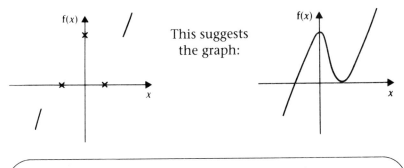

This suggests the graph:

(a) How can you obtain facts (i) and (ii) in the solution to example 2 *without* multiplying out the brackets?

(b) Why is 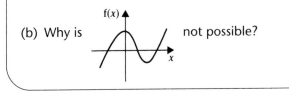 not possible?

> You can get a good idea of the main features of the graph of
> a polynomial function, f(x), by
>
> (a) knowing the zeros, i.e. where it cuts the x-axis;
>
> (b) knowing f(0), i.e. where it cuts the y-axis;
>
> (c) applying the principles of dominance.
>
> It is only necessary to apply those principles which enable
> the essential features of the curve to be drawn.

EXERCISE 3

1 For the function $f(x) = (x - 2)(x + 3)(3x - 7)$, which in expanded form is

$$f(x) = 3x^3 - 4x^2 - 25x + 42$$

(a) on a partial sketch:

(i) mark any zeros on a set of axes;

(ii) mark the value of f(x) when $x = 0$;

(iii) sketch the dominant parts of the graph;

(b) complete the sketch.

2 For the function

$$f(x) = -5x^4 + 28x^3 - 33x^2 + 2x + 8$$

(a) sketch the dominant parts of the graph;

(b) complete the sketch.

3 Sketch the graph of the function

$$y = x^3(x + 4)(x - 7)$$

4

A girl standing on the edge of a cliff throws a stone. The height of the stone above the point of release, after t seconds, is given by

$$h = t(12 - 5t) \text{ metres}$$

(a) When is the stone level with the point of release again?

(b) The stone hits the sea after 4 seconds. Estimate the height of the cliff above sea level.

(c) Sketch a graph of height against time.

After working through this chapter you should:

1 understand the meaning of the term function;

2 be able to define and describe a function using the correct notation;

3 be able to sketch the graphs of functions using

(a) zeros;

(b) dominance.

Translations

Help is given on Technology datasheet: *Plotting graphs*.

1 (a) Sketch the graph of $f(x) = x^2$.

   (b) Rearrange the expression for $f(x - 2) + 5$ into the form $ax^2 + bx + c$.

   (c) Superimpose the graph of $f(x - 2) + 5$. How is this related to the graph of $f(x)$?

2 For each of the following functions

   (a) $g(x) = x^3$ (b) $g(x) = 2^x$ (c) $g(x) = \sqrt{x}$

    (i) sketch the graph of $g(x)$;

    (ii) write down the expression for $g(x - 2) + 5$;

    (iii) what translation of the graph of $g(x)$ would you expect?

    (iv) superimpose the graph of $g(x - 2) + 5$ and check your answer to part (iii).

3 (a) Sketch the graph of $f(x) = |x|$.

   (b) Without using a graph plotter, sketch the graph of $|x + 3| - 4$.

   (c) Check your answer using a graph plotter.

4 (a) For any function f, what is the relationship between the graph of $f(x)$ and $f(x + a) + b$?

   (b) Illustrate your answer to (a) by choosing your own function and values for a and b.

   (c) Will what you have described be true for any function?

5E (a) Investigate the relationship between $g(x)$ and $g(x + a) + b$ when $g(x) = \sin x$.

   (b) Write an illustrated account of your findings.

6E (a) Investigate the relationships between the graphs of

        $h(x)$ and $ah(bx + c) + d$

   where h is any function and a, b, c, d may take any values.

   (b) Write an illustrated account of your findings.

Dominance

On this tasksheet you may find that your initial choice of axes will fail to show a given property. In such cases, you will need to redraw the axes to stretch or shrink the graph in the x- or y-direction. When this happens, remember to ask yourself why your initial choice was mistaken.

1 (a) Plot on the same screen and thus superimpose each of the following graphs.

  (i) $y = x^2$ (ii) $y = x^3$ (iii) $y = x^4$ (iv) $y = x^5$

  (b) What points do all the graphs have in common?

  (c) Which function increases most rapidly, and which increases least rapidly, as x becomes large?

  (d) What are the main differences between the graphs of the even powers of x and the graphs of odd powers of x?

2 (a) Plot on the same screen the following graphs:

  (i) $y = x^2$ (ii) $y = 4x$ (iii) $y = x^2 + 4x$

  (b) What do you notice about the graphs of $y = x^2$ and $y = x^2 + 4x$ when x is a large positive or negative number?

  (c) What do you notice about the graphs of $y = 4x$ and $y = x^2 + 4x$ when x is a small positive or negative number?

3 (a) Plot on the same screen the following graphs:

  (i) $y = x^3$ (ii) $y = -4x^2$ (iii) $y = x^3 - 4x^2$

  (b) What do you notice about the graphs of $y = -4x^2$ and $y = x^3 - 4x^2$ when x is a small positive or negative number?

  (c) What do you notice about the graphs of $y = x^3$ and $y = x^3 - 4x^2$ when x is a large positive or negative number?

4 (a) Plot the graph of the function
$y = x^3 + x^2 - 2x + 1$.

  (b) Superimpose the graphs of

  (i) $y = x^3$ (ii) $y = -2x + 1$

  (c) Compare the three graphs for

  (i) large positive and negative values of x;

  (ii) very small positive and negative values of x.

  (d) Suggest a reason for ignoring the terms x^2, $-2x$ and 1 when considering the shape of the graph in part (a) for large values of x.

  (e) Suggest a reason for ignoring the terms x^3 and x^2 when considering the shape of the graph in part (a) for very small values of x.

5 Plot the graph of the function $y = 3x + 2x^2 - x^3$.
What are the zeros of this function; that is, where does the graph cross the x-axis?
Which term do you think determines the shape for:

(a) large positive and negative values of x;

(b) very small positive and negative values of x?

6 (a) What term is suggested by the shape of the graph when x is large?

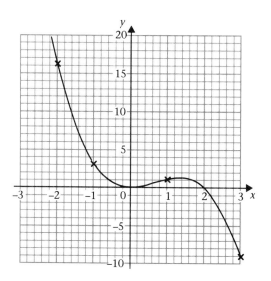

(b) What term is suggested by the shape of the graph when x is small?

(c) (i) Suggest an equation for the graph above.

(ii) To confirm your suggestion, plot the graph of your equation.

(d) If necessary repeat (c) until you have found the equation of the graph.

4 Expressions and equations

4.1 The language of algebra

The standard A sizes for paper are designed so that when a sheet of paper is cut in half, the two halves are similar in shape to the original. Thus, when a sheet of A4 paper is halved two sheets of A5 are produced.

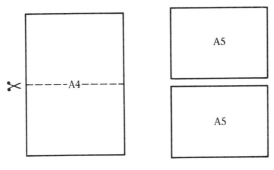

(a) Suppose that an A4 sheet has width 1 unit and length l units. What are the dimensions of an A5 sheet?

(b) Determine the value of l and check your result with the actual dimensions of A4 and A5 paper.

(c) The A0 size has an area of 1 m². What is the area of the A4 size? Verify your answer by measurement.

In the example above, the letter l was used to represent an **unknown quantity**. The information was then written mathematically as an equation and the problem was solved by using familiar algebraic techniques to solve the equation.

As well as using letters to represent unknowns, you can use letters to state **general** results such as

$$1 + 2 + \ldots + n = \frac{n(n+1)}{2}$$

for the sum of a simple arithmetic progression.

Letters can also stand for **variables** in algebraic expressions.

(a) In the expression

$$y = ax^2 + bx + c$$

x is called the **independent** variable and y is called the **dependent** variable. What is meant by this?

(b) The letters a and x are both in the formula for y. In what way do they play different roles?

The algebraic statement

$$x^2 + 3x + 2 = (x + 1)(x + 2)$$

is called an **identity**.

How does an identity differ from an equation?

Many problems must be expressed algebraically before they can be solved mathematically. This will often lead to an equation which needs to be solved.

A review of some methods of solving algebraic equations is given in tasksheet 1S and some examples of formulating and solving equations are given in tasksheet 1.

T A S K S H E E T   1   o r   1 S   –   Solving problems (page 88) or
Review of equations (page 89)

E X E R C I S E   1

1 Solve the equations

(a) $3x + 9 = 0$ (b) $x^2 = 25$ (c) $x^2 + 5x - 6 = 0$

(d) $x = \dfrac{4}{x}$ (e) $4(x + 3) = 6(2 - x)$ (f) $x(x - 4) = 0$

2 The triangular numbers are defined as

$T_1 = 1$ $T_2 = 1 + 2$ $T_3 = 1 + 2 + 3$ etc.

If the nth triangular number is 210:

(a) formulate an equation for n;

(b) solve this equation to find n.

4.2 Quadratic equations

The path round the square lawn is 1 metre wide. If the area of the path is equal to the area of the lawn, the dimensions of the lawn may be found as follows .

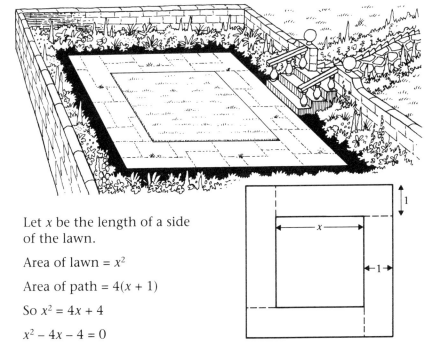

Let x be the length of a side of the lawn.

Area of lawn = x^2

Area of path = $4(x + 1)$

So $x^2 = 4x + 4$

$x^2 - 4x - 4 = 0$

This equation does not factorise to give integer roots!

> Express $x^2 - 4x - 4$ in completed square form. Hence solve $x^2 - 4x - 4 = 0$.

Using the completed square form gives an alternative approach to solving a quadratic equation. It can also be used to derive an important formula that can be applied to any quadratic.

TASKSHEET 2 – Quadratic equations (page 91)

> The formula for solving the general quadratic equation $ax^2 + bx + c = 0$, $a \neq 0$, is
>
> $$x = \frac{-b \pm \sqrt{b^2 - 4ac}}{2a}$$

EXAMPLE 1

Solve the equation $5x^2 - 3x - 4 = 0$, giving the solutions correct to 2 decimal places.

SOLUTION

Using $x = \dfrac{-b \pm \sqrt{b^2 - 4ac}}{2a}$, where $a = 5$, $b = -3$, $c = -4$,

$$x = \frac{3 \pm \sqrt{9 - 4 \times 5 \times (-4)}}{2 \times 5}$$

$$\Rightarrow x = \frac{3 \pm \sqrt{89}}{10}$$

$\Rightarrow x = 1.24$ or $x = -0.64$ (to 2 decimal places)

Note that the solution may be given in one of two forms:

$\dfrac{3 \pm \sqrt{89}}{10}$ are the **exact** solutions;

1.24 or -0.64 are the **approximate** solutions, written to 2 decimal places.

EXERCISE 2

1 Use the quadratic equation formula to solve the following, giving your answers (a) in exact form, and (b) to 2 decimal places.

   (i) $x^2 + 5x + 3 = 0$ (ii) $3x^2 + 6x + 2 = 0$

   (iii) $3x^2 + 4x - 1 = 0$ (iv) $5x^2 - 8x - 1 = 0$

   (v) $-2x^2 + 7x + 1 = 0$

2 Rearrange the following equations and then solve them, giving your answers to 2 decimal places.

   (a) $x^2 + 2x = 4$ (b) $5x^2 = 3x + 4$

   (c) $8 = 7x - x^2$ (d) $6x^2 + 10x - 4 = x^2 + 7x - 3$

3 Solve the following equations where possible, giving your answers to 2 decimal places. Use factors, where appropriate, otherwise use either the formula or completing the square.

   (a) $8x - x^2 = 0$ (b) $x^2 + 2x = 5x + 4$

   (c) $x^2 + x - 1 = 0$ (d) $x^2 = 25$

   (e) $x^2 + x + 1 = 0$ (f) $25 = 10x - x^2$

4

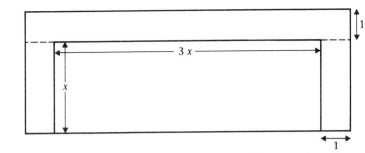

A rectangular lawn which is three times as wide as it is long has a 1 metre path round three sides only, as shown above. The area of the path is equal to the area of the lawn.

(a) If the dimensions of the lawn are x metres × $3x$ metres as shown, explain why

$$3x^2 = 5x + 2$$

(b) Hence find the dimensions of the lawn.

5 Two numbers differ by 1 and have a product of 10. Let n be the smaller number.

(a) Explain why

$$n^2 + n - 10 = 0$$

(b) Hence find the two numbers exactly.

6 (a) Use the formula to solve, where possible, the equation $f(x) = 0$ for each of the functions

(i) $f(x) = x^2 - 2x + 4$

(ii) $f(x) = x^2 - 4x + 4$

(iii) $f(x) = x^2 - 6x + 4$

(b) The graph of each of the functions is given below. Use the information about the roots that you found in part (a) to match each function to its graph.

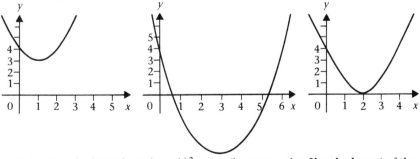

(c) Describe how the value of $b^2 - 4ac$ (known as the **discriminant** of the quadratic equation) relates to the number of roots.

T A S K S H E E T 3E – Regular pentagons and the Fibonacci sequence (page 92)

4.3 Inequalities

Some problems may not lead to an equation, but may give rise to an inequality.

> What is the first triangular number greater than 50?

Trial and error may lead you to the result that $n = 10$, but if you were to take an algebraic approach you would have to solve

$$1 + 2 + 3 + \ldots + n > 50$$

$$\frac{n(n+1)}{2} > 50$$

$$n^2 + n - 100 > 0$$

which is an example of a quadratic inequality.

We shall give two examples of how to handle inequalities. The first demonstrates how to solve a linear inequality.

E X A M P L E   2

Find the solution set for the inequality $t + 2 > 6t + 7$

> What is meant by a solution set?

S O L U T I O N

$$t + 2 > 6t + 7$$

$\Rightarrow -5t > 5$ Step 1:   Gather together like terms.

$\Rightarrow \quad t < -1$ Step 2:   Divide both sides by a negative value (note the change in the inequality sign).

 T A S K S H E E T   4S   —   Handling inequalities (page 99)

When manipulating inequalities algebraically, normal algebraic rules are obeyed, except that when both sides are multiplied or divided by a negative number the inequality sign is reversed.

A graphical approach is helpful in solving quadratic inequalities.

The graph of $y = (x + 1)(x - 2)$ is as shown.

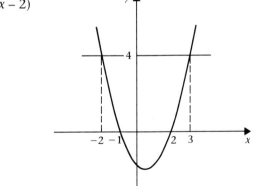

(a) Find the solution set for the following inequalities:

    (i) $(x + 1)(x - 2) > 0$

    (ii) $(x + 1)(x - 2) > 4$

(b) Find the first triangular number greater than 100.

When you solve a quadratic inequality you are seeking the set of values for which it is true. It is usually simplest to solve the corresponding **equation** and refer to a sketch graph to find the ranges of values which satisfy the inequality.

E X A M P L E 3

For what values of x is

(a) $x^2 > 6 - x$

(b) $x^2 < 6 - x$?

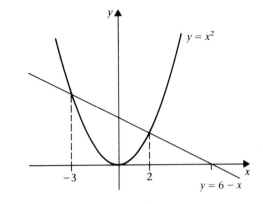

S O L U T I O N

Solving

$$x^2 = 6 - x$$

$$x^2 + x - 6 = 0$$

$$(x + 3)(x - 2) = 0$$

$$x = -3 \text{ or } x = 2$$

From the graph you can see that

(a) $x^2 > 6 - x$ when **either** $x < -3$ **or** $x > 2$.

(b) $x^2 < 6 - x$ when **both** $x > -3$ **and** $x < 2$. This solution set is usually written as $-3 < x < 2$.

> By sketching an appropriate graph, solve the cubic inequality
>
> $$(x + 1)(x - 2)(x - 4) \leq 0$$

EXERCISE 3

1 Solve

(a) $5x < -10$ (b) $1 - 2x < 3x + 6$

(c) $2(x - 3) < 8$ (d) $3(x + 5) < 2x + 3$

(e) $-3x < 6$

2 Find the range of possible values for x if $(2 - x)^2 > 0$.

3

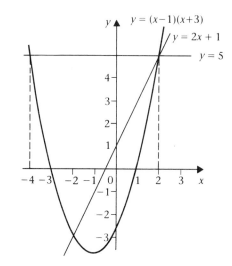

Use the graph to write down the solutions of

(a) $(x - 1)(x + 3) \leq 0$ (b) $(x - 1)(x + 3) > 5$ (c) $(x - 1)(x + 3) < 2x + 1$

4 Use sketch graphs to help solve the inequalities

(a) $(x + 5)(x - 2) > 0$ (b) $(x - 2)(3 - x) \leq 0$

(c) $(x + 2)(x - 2)(x - 5) \geq 0$ (d) $(x + 2)(x - 2)^2 \geq 0$

5 Solve the inequalities

(a) $x^2 < 3x$ (b) $3x^2 + 2x \leq 2x^2 + 3x$

(c) $x(x - 3) < 10$ (d) $x^2 + x > 1$

6 Find the first triangular number which is greater than 1000.

4.4 Polynomials

A **polynomial** is a function involving whole number powers of a variable. In general, you can write

$$P(x) = a_0 + a_1 x + a_2 x^2 + a_3 x^3 + \ldots + a_n x^n$$

where $a_0, a_1, a_2, \ldots, a_n$ are constants, referred to as **coefficients**. The highest power present is the **degree** of the polynomial. For example, a cubic polynomial is a polynomial of degree 3, such as

$$P(x) = x^3 + 3x^2 - 6x - 8$$

> Check that $(x + 1)(x - 2)(x + 4) = x^3 + 3x^2 - 6x - 8$

T A S K S H E E T   5S – Expanding brackets (page 101)

How are the zeros of $P(x)$ related to the factors?

By looking for the zeros of a polynomial you will quickly discover whether or not it has a simple factor. Tasksheet 6 shows you how to find further factors.

T A S K S H E E T   6   –   Factorising polynomials (page 102)

The properties and methods obtained so far may be summarised by **the factor theorem**.

> If $x = a$ is a solution of the polynomial equation $P(x) = 0$, then $x - a$ is a factor of $P(x)$.
>
> $P(x)$ can then be rewritten as $(x - a)Q(x)$ where $Q(x)$ is a 'simpler' polynomial.

The factorised form of a polynomial $P(x)$ is very convenient for solving the equation $P(x) = 0$ and for sketching the graph of $P(x)$.

EXAMPLE 4

For the function $f(x) = x^3 - 3x^2 - 10x + 24$:

(a) find the factors of $f(x)$;

(b) find the roots of the equation $f(x) = 0$;

(c) sketch the graph of $f(x)$.

SOLUTION

(a) The possible factors of 24 are $\pm1, \pm2, \pm3, \pm4, \pm6, \pm8, \pm12$ and ±24.

   By trial,

   $f(2) = 8 - 12 - 20 + 24 = 0$,

   so

   $x - 2$ is a factor.

   Therefore, you can write $x^3 - 3x^2 - 10x + 24$ as $(x - 2)(x^2 + ax - 12)$.

   Comparing the coefficients of x^2 gives

   $$-3 = -2 + a$$

   $$\Rightarrow a = -1$$

   and so

   $$f(x) = (x - 2)(x^2 - x - 12)$$

   $$= (x - 2)(x + 3)(x - 4)$$

(b) $f(x) = 0$

   $$\Rightarrow (x - 2)(x + 3)(x - 4) = 0$$

   $$\Rightarrow x = -3, 2, 4$$

(c) The graph is a cubic which cuts the x-axis at -3, 2, 4 and the y-axis at 24 as shown.

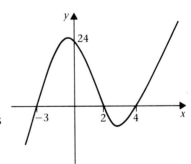

EXERCISE 4

1   If $P(x) = x^3 - 2x^2 - 11x + 12$

   (a) show that $x + 3$ is a factor of $P(x)$;

   (b) find $Q(x)$, if $P(x) = (x + 3)Q(x)$.

2   If $P(x) = x^3 - 5x^2 + 2x + 8$

(a)   use the factor theorem to find one factor of $P(x)$;

(b)   factorise $P(x)$ completely;

(c)   write down the solutions of $P(x) = 0$;

(d)   sketch the graph of $P(x)$.

3   Solve the equation $x^3 + 5x^2 + 3x - 9 = 0$.

4   Solve the equation $x^3 + 4x^2 + 2x - 4 = 0$ by finding one simple factor and then solving a quadratic equation.

5   (a)   Solve the equation $x^3 - 2x + 4 = 0$.

(b)   Sketch a graph of the function to explain the solution.

6   (a)   Find all the zeros and hence factorise the function
$$P(x) = x^4 - x^3 - 7x^2 + x + 6$$

(b)   Sketch the graph of the function.

(c)   Solve the inequality $P(x) > 0$.

7   (a)   What happens if you try to factorise completely:
(i) $x^3 - 8$
(ii) $x^4 - 16$

(b)   Sketch the graphs of these functions and comment on their zeros.

After working through this chapter you should:

1   understand the terms identity, root, polynomial, coefficient;

2   understand that a letter can be used in algebra to generalise, to stand for a variable or a constant, or to represent an unknown quantity;

3   be able to formulate equations for a given problem;

4   be able to solve any quadratic equation;

5   be able to find the solution set for simple polynomial inequalities;

6   know how to use the factor theorem to help solve polynomial equations.

Solving problems

1 (a) Find the sum of three consecutive numbers. Repeat for several other sets of three consecutive numbers. What do you notice about the results?

   (b) Any three consecutive numbers can be written algebraically as:

   $$n, (n + 1), (n + 2)$$

   Find the sum of these 3 algebraic terms. How does this explain what you have observed about the numerical results?

In question 1, the letter n is used to represent a **general** number, to prove a result that is true for **all** numbers. In other examples a letter is used to stand for a specific, **unknown** number in which an equation is set up and then solved.

2 'The difference between the squares of two consecutive odd numbers is always a multiple of 8.'

   (a) Test this result in a few numerical cases. Is it true for the odd numbers

   91 378 627 513 and 91 378 627 515?

   (b) Prove the result algebraically.

3

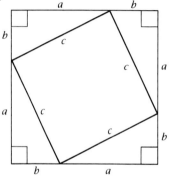

'A bamboo 18 cubits high was broken by the wind. Its top touched the ground 6 cubits from the root. Tell the lengths of the segments of the bamboo.'

Solve this problem posed by Brahmagupta (Hindu mathematician c.AD 630)

(from H. Eves, *Introduction to the History of Mathematics*)

4 4 right-angled triangles with sides a, b, and c are arranged as shown in the diagram.

Explain why the area of the large square can be given as both $(a + b)^2$ and $c^2 + 2ab$.

Use these two results to prove Pythagoras' Theorem.

Review of equations

You have already met several types of algebraic equation. This tasksheet reviews methods of solving such equations and gives you an opportunity for further practice.

Linear equations

EXAMPLE

Solve $6x + 14 = 2x - 6$.

SOLUTION

$6x = 2x - 20$ (subtracting 14 from both sides)

$\Rightarrow 4x = -20$ (subtracting $2x$ from both sides)

$\Rightarrow x = -5$ (dividing both sides by 4)

1 Solve

(a) $5x + 30 = 0$

(b) $4x + 3 = 2x$

(c) $5x + 2 = 3x - 7$

(d) $4(x - 3) = 6x$

(e) $3(2x + 5) = 3(x + 2)$

(f) $x + 4 = 3 - 2x$

Quadratic equations

EXAMPLE

Solve the equation $x^2 + 6x - 7 = 0$.

SOLUTION

$x^2 + 6x - 7 = 0$

$\Rightarrow (x - 1)(x + 7) = 0$

$\Rightarrow$ either $x - 1 = 0$ or $x + 7 = 0$

$\Rightarrow x = 1$ or $x = -7$

2 Solve

(a) $(x - 3)(x + 5) = 0$

(b) $x(x - 2) = 0$

(c) $x^2 + 3x - 18 = 0$

(d) $x^2 - 3x - 10 = 0$

(e) $x^2 - 4x = 0$

(f) $x^2 - 6x + 9 = 0$

Other methods

Some equations can be solved by inspection, though care sometimes needs to be taken not to miss solutions – for example, $x^2 = 9$ clearly has $x = 3$ as a solution, but it also has the solution $x = -3$.

Other equations may need some rearrangement before solving.

E X A M P L E

Solve the equation $x = \dfrac{16}{x}$.

S O L U T I O N

$$x = \frac{16}{x}$$

$\Rightarrow x^2 = 16$ (multiplying both sides by x)

$\Rightarrow x = \pm 4$

3 Solve

(a) $x^2 = 49$

(b) $x^2 - 9 = 0$

(c) $x = \dfrac{9}{x}$

(d) $x^2 + 2x = 35$

(e) $x^2 = 5x$

(f) $x - \dfrac{1}{x} = 0$

Quadratic equations

1   Solve the equation $x^2 + 6x + 4 = 0$ using the method of completing the square.

The solution of the equation $x^2 + bx + c = 0$ depends entirely on the two numbers b and c. You can find a formula for the solutions in terms of these two letters using the method of completing the square.

$$x^2 + bx + c = 0$$

$$\left(x + \frac{b}{2}\right)^2 - \frac{b^2}{4} + c = 0 \qquad \text{①}$$

$$\left(x + \frac{b}{2}\right)^2 = \frac{b^2}{4} - c \qquad \text{②}$$

$$\left(x + \frac{b}{2}\right)^2 = \frac{b^2 - 4c}{4} \qquad \text{③}$$

$$x + \frac{b}{2} = \frac{\pm\sqrt{b^2 - 4c}}{2} \qquad \text{④}$$

$$x = \frac{-b \pm \sqrt{b^2 - 4c}}{2}$$

2 (a) Explain where the $\dfrac{b^2}{4}$ has come from in line ①.

   (b) Why has the c in line ② become $4c$ in line ③?

   (c) Why has the $\pm$ appeared in line ④?

3 Use the formula to solve

   (a) $x^2 + 6x + 4 = 0$ (b) $x^2 - 6x + 4 = 0$ (c) $x^2 = 5 - 3x$

> By using a method similar to that in question 1, it can be shown that the solution to the general quadratic equation $ax^2 + bx + c = 0$ is
>
> $$x = \frac{-b \pm \sqrt{b^2 - 4ac}}{2a}$$

4 For the following quadratic equations, write down the values of a, b and c which must be used in the formula above. Hence solve each of the equations giving your answers correct to 2 decimal places.

   (a) $x^2 - 4x - 4 = 0$ (b) $3x^2 - 7x - 2 = 0$ (c) $3x^2 = 4x + 1$

5E Obtain the formula

$$x = \frac{-b \pm \sqrt{b^2 - 4ac}}{2a}$$

Regular pentagons and the Fibonacci sequence

1 Why is the interior angle of a regular pentagon 108°?

If you have ever tried to draw a regular pentagon of given edge length, you will have found that it is difficult to get an accurate diagram if you use a method that involves measuring the interior angles of 108° with a protractor.

A better method would involve measuring lengths only, using compasses to construct the diagram. To do this you need to know the length of the diagonals of a regular pentagon. The procedure for drawing the pentagon is then as shown below, where the edge length is 1 and the diagonal length is denoted by the Greek letter ϕ ('phi').

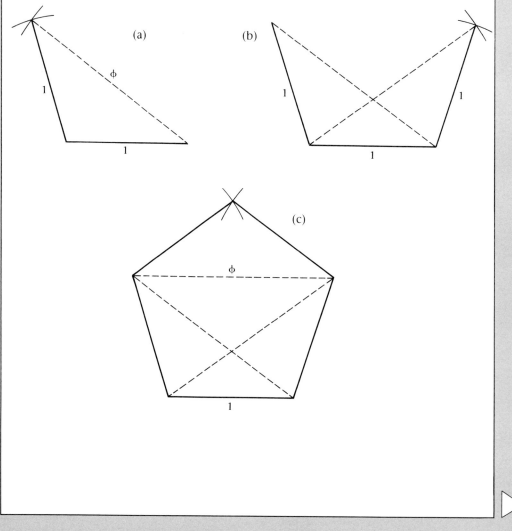

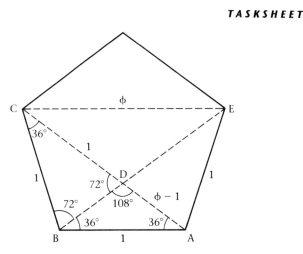

ϕ can be calculated using the fact that triangle CDE is an enlargement of triangle ABD with ϕ as the scale factor. Since it is a diagonal, AC = ϕ. Also CD = 1, so AD = $\phi - 1$. By comparing the sides AD and CD in triangles ABD and CDE, it then follows that

$$\phi(\phi - 1) = 1 \qquad \text{①}$$

---

2 Explain the values for the angles in triangle ABC.

3 Explain why CD = 1 and $\phi(\phi - 1) = 1$.

Rearranging ① gives: $\phi^2 - \phi - 1 = 0$

$$\left(\phi - \frac{1}{2}\right)^2 - \frac{5}{4} = 0$$

$$\phi = \frac{1}{2}(1 + \sqrt{5}) \text{ or } \phi = \frac{1}{2}(1 - \sqrt{5})$$

$$\phi \approx 1.618 \qquad \text{or } \phi \approx -0.618 \text{ (to 3 d.p.)}$$

As far as the diagonal of the regular pentagon is concerned, the negative root is meaningless, so the diagonal length is 1.618, or, perhaps more usefully, the diagonal length is the edge length multiplied by 1.618. You now have a simpler means of calculating the diagonal for a given edge and then drawing an accurate regular pentagon.

---

4 Give full details of how the method of completing the square is used to solve the following equation to 3 decimal places:

$$\phi^2 - \phi - 1 = 0$$

5 Using a suitable diagonal length, draw accurately a regular pentagon with 5 cm edges.

The story does not end at this point, because regular pentagons can be enlarged by extending pairs of sides and joining the five points of intersection, as illustrated below.

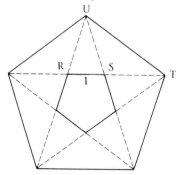

Two of the outer triangles making up the shape above are shown below.

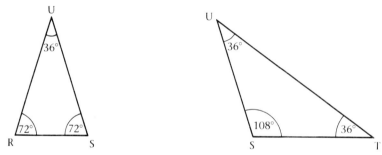

These triangles are similar to those used on page 93 and so

$$SU = \phi \times RS = \phi$$
$$UT = \phi \times SU = \phi^2$$

---

6   Explain why SU = ϕ and UT = ϕ^2.

The edge length of the larger pentagon is ϕ^2. Moreover, the diagonal of the larger pentagon must be ϕ^3. So you can see the striking fact that the sequence of lengths

> edge, diagonal, edge, diagonal, . . .

for a succession of regular pentagons, formed by extending the sides, takes the form of a simple geometric sequence

> $1, \phi, \phi^2, \phi^3, \ldots$

---

7   Why is a diagonal of the larger pentagon given by ϕ^3?

Previously, the value of ϕ has been calculated as $\frac{1}{2}(1 + \sqrt{5})$. It is interesting to examine the sequence of powers of ϕ expressed in surd form.

$$\phi = \frac{1}{2}(1 + \sqrt{5}) \qquad\qquad \phi^4 = \frac{1}{2}(7 + 3\sqrt{5})$$

$$\phi^2 = \frac{1}{2}(3 + \sqrt{5}) \qquad\qquad \phi^5 = \frac{1}{2}(11 + 5\sqrt{5})$$

$$\phi^3 = \frac{1}{2}(4 + 2\sqrt{5}) \qquad\qquad \phi^6 = \frac{1}{2}(18 + 8\sqrt{5})$$

---

8 ϕ^2 is calculated from $\phi = \frac{1}{2}(1 + \sqrt{5})$ by multiplying out brackets and simplifying as follows.

$$\phi = \frac{1}{2}(1 + \sqrt{5}) \times \frac{1}{2}(1 + \sqrt{5})$$

$$\phi = \frac{1}{4}(1 + \sqrt{5} + \sqrt{5} + 5)$$

$$\phi = \frac{1}{4}(6 + 2\sqrt{5})$$

$$\phi = \frac{1}{2}(3 + \sqrt{5})$$

Check the values for ϕ^3 up to ϕ^6 in the same way and calculate ϕ^7 and ϕ^8.

Two important sequences are known as the **Lucas sequence**

$$1, 3, 4, 7, 11, 18, \ldots$$

and the **Fibonacci** sequence

$$1, 1, 2, 3, 5, 8, \ldots$$

In both sequences, successive terms are found by adding the two previous terms.

We next consider how you can find formulas for the general terms of these two sequences.

When ϕ was calculated there was a second root, $\frac{1}{2}(1 - \sqrt{5})$, which will now be referred to as ψ ('psi'). This generates a sequence similar to that for ϕ. The two sequences are placed alongside each other for comparison.

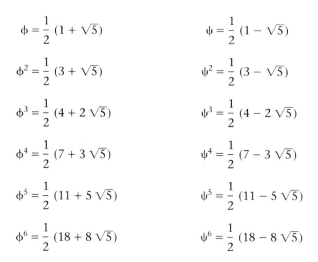

$$\phi = \frac{1}{2}(1 + \sqrt{5}) \qquad \psi = \frac{1}{2}(1 - \sqrt{5})$$

$$\phi^2 = \frac{1}{2}(3 + \sqrt{5}) \qquad \psi^2 = \frac{1}{2}(3 - \sqrt{5})$$

$$\phi^3 = \frac{1}{2}(4 + 2\sqrt{5}) \qquad \psi^3 = \frac{1}{2}(4 - 2\sqrt{5})$$

$$\phi^4 = \frac{1}{2}(7 + 3\sqrt{5}) \qquad \psi^4 = \frac{1}{2}(7 - 3\sqrt{5})$$

$$\phi^5 = \frac{1}{2}(11 + 5\sqrt{5}) \qquad \psi^5 = \frac{1}{2}(11 - 5\sqrt{5})$$

$$\phi^6 = \frac{1}{2}(18 + 8\sqrt{5}) \qquad \psi^6 = \frac{1}{2}(18 - 8\sqrt{5})$$

If you add corresponding members of the two sequences you obtain the Lucas sequence. The Fibonacci sequence is obtained by subtracting corresponding members and then dividing by $\sqrt{5}$.

$$\phi + \psi = 1 \qquad \phi - \psi = \sqrt{5}$$

$$\phi^2 + \psi^2 = 3 \qquad \phi^2 - \psi^2 = \sqrt{5}$$

$$\phi^3 + \psi^3 = 4 \qquad \phi^3 - \psi^3 = 2\sqrt{5}$$

$$\phi^4 + \psi^4 = 7 \qquad \phi^4 - \psi^4 = 3\sqrt{5}$$

$$\phi^5 + \psi^5 = 11 \qquad \phi^5 - \psi^5 = 5\sqrt{5}$$

$$\phi^6 + \psi^6 = 18 \qquad \phi^6 - \psi^6 = 8\sqrt{5}$$

You now have formulas for the general or nth terms, L_n and F_n, of the Lucas and Fibonacci sequences:

$$L_n = \phi^n + \psi^n$$

$$= \left[\frac{1}{2}(1 + \sqrt{5})\right]^n + \left[\frac{1}{2}(1 - \sqrt{5})\right]^n ;$$

$$F_n = \frac{1}{\sqrt{5}}(\phi^n - \psi^n) = \frac{1}{\sqrt{5}}\left[\left(\frac{1}{2}(1 + \sqrt{5})\right)^n - \left(\frac{1}{2}(1 - \sqrt{5})\right)^n\right]$$

9 Verify that $\phi^7 + \psi^7$ and $\dfrac{1}{\sqrt{5}}\,(\phi^7 + \psi^7)$ give the seventh terms of the Lucas

and Fibonacci sequences and verify the eighth terms in the same way.

10 Use a calculator or computer to tabulate ϕ^n, ψ^n, L_n and F_n for a range of values of n. In particular observe the behaviour of ψ^n.

It is instructive to look at the four sequences ϕ^n, ψ^n, L_n and F_n numerically, using a calculator or a simple program on a microcomputer. In particular, it will be noted that the terms of ψ^n rapidly become small because ψ is numerically less than 1. The first terms in the formulas for L_n and F_n give approximations to the sequences, which improve in accuracy as n gets larger.

The approximations are

$$L_n \approx \left(\frac{1}{2}\,(1 + \sqrt{5}) \right)^n$$

$$F_n \approx \frac{1}{\sqrt{5}} \left(\frac{1}{2}\,(1 + \sqrt{5}) \right)^n$$

11 Calculate the ratios of successive pairs of terms in each sequence. In other words, calculate

$$\frac{L_n}{L_{n-1}} \quad \text{and} \quad \frac{F_n}{F_{n-1}}$$

What do you notice and how can this be explained in relation to the approximations of L_n and F_n?

The Greeks derived ϕ from the **golden rectangle**, which was thought to display particularly pleasing proportions, and is, for example, the shape used for the frontage of the Parthenon in Athens. ϕ is known as the **golden ratio**, the ratio of the sides of a golden rectangle. A golden rectangle is such that when a square of the same width is removed the remaining rectangle is also golden, as shown below.

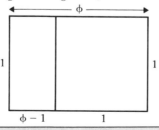

Since the length of the golden rectangle is the width multiplied by ϕ, it follows that

$$\phi (\phi - 1) = 1$$
$$\phi^2 - \phi - 1 = 0$$

which is precisely the equation derived earlier in relation to the diagonal length of a regular pentagon.

These two sources of the golden ratio – the regular pentagon and the golden rectangle – are brought together very nicely in the regular icosahedron. The icosahedron is a regular polyhedron with twenty faces in the form of equilateral triangles. If three golden rectangles are fitted together so that they are mutually perpendicular, their twelve vertices form the vertices of a regular icosahedron.

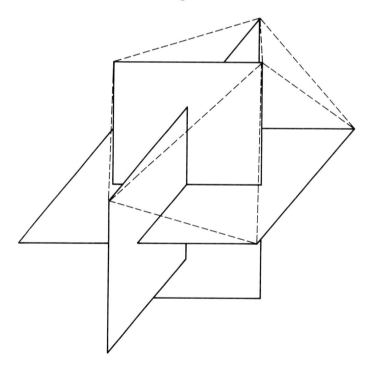

In this icosahedron, five equilateral triangles meet at a vertex. Such a set of triangles forms a pyramid with a regular pentagon as its base. One of these pentagonal pyramids is shown by the dotted lines above. Note that the edges of the icosahedron are the same length as the shorter edges of the golden rectangles and that the one diagonal of the regular pentagon that is shown is the longer edge of one of the golden rectangles. So the icosahedron provides a link between regular pentagons and golden rectangles.

Handling inequalities

1 Find the solution set for

$$t + 3 > 5 \quad \text{①}$$

(a) (geometrically)

By studying the graphs, find the values of t for which statement ① is true.

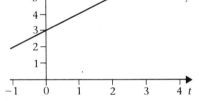

(b) (algebraically)

(i) If $t = 4$ is statement ① true?

(ii) Try the whole numbers from -5 to 5. For which of these values of t is statement ① true?

(iii) The solution set for ① is

$$t > \text{_____} \ .$$

2 By testing with whole numbers, copy and complete the following.

(a) If $x - 4 > -3$ then $x > \text{_____}$.

(b) If $4x > 12$ then $x > \text{_____}$.

3 (a) By testing with whole numbers copy and complete the following.
If $-3x > 6$ then $x \text{_____}$.

(b) State in your own words what happened in part (a).

(c) (i) Is the following solution correct?

$$2x - 5 > 5x + 1$$
$$-3x > 6$$
$$-x > 2$$
$$x < -2$$

(ii) Write down some numbers which are in the solution set.

3 (continued)

(d) Using the graph below explain why the solution set for $2x - 5 > 5x + 1$ is $x < -2$.

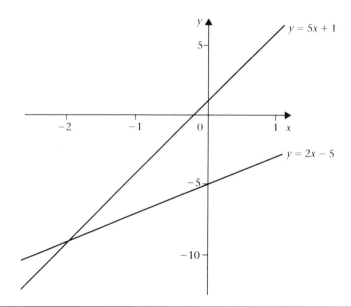

When manipulating inequalities algebraically, normal algebraic rules are obeyed except that when both sides are multiplied or divided by a negative number the inequality sign is reversed.

4 Find the solution sets for

(a) $5x + 1 < 2x + 7$ (b) $2x - 1 > 5 - x$

(c) $1 - 2x < x - 7$ (d) $3 > 1 + 2x$

(e) $1 - \frac{1}{3} x < 4$ (f) $3 - 2x > 2 - 3x$

Expanding brackets

When multiplying out more than two brackets, a well organised methodical and careful approach is important if careless mistakes are to be avoided.

With three sets of brackets

$(x - 1)(x + 3)(x - 4)$

$= (x - 1)(x^2 - x - 12)$	Expand brackets in pairs only.
$= x(x^2 - x - 12) - (x^2 - x - 12)$	This may be omitted, but errors with signs are common and this is when they usually occur.
$= x^3 - x^2 - 12x - x^2 + x + 12$	Gather together like terms.
$= x^3 - 2x^2 - 11x + 12$	

1 Expand

(a) $(x - 1)(x^2 + x + 1)$ (b) $(x - 2)(x^2 + 2x + 4)$

(c) $(x + 1)(x^2 - x + 1)$ (d) $(x + 2)(x^2 - 2x + 4)$

2 Expand

(a) $(x + 1)(x + 2)(x - 4)$ (b) $(x - 2)(x - 3)(x - 4)$

(c) $(x - 1)(x + 1)(x + 5)$ (d) $(x - 1)^2(x + 3)$

With more than three sets of brackets

$(x + 1)(x - 2)(x + 2)(x - 3)$

$= (x + 1)(x^2 - 4)(x - 3)$	The pairs of brackets may be expanded in any order. Your experience might help you to speed up the process by choosing a convenient pair.
$= (x + 1)(x^3 - 3x^2 - 4x + 12)$	
$= x^4 - 3x^3 - 4x^2 + 12x$ $\quad + x^3 - 3x^2 - 4x + 12$	Careful setting out makes any simplification easy.
$= x^4 - 2x^3 - 7x^2 + 8x + 12$	

3 Expand

(a) $(x + 1)(x - 1)(x + 2)(x - 2)$ (b) $(x + 2)^2(x - 2)^2$

(c) $(x - 1)(x + 3)^3$ (d) $(x + 1)(x - 2)(x + 3)(x - 4)$

Factorising polynomials

1 For the polynomial

$$P(x) = x^3 - 13x - 12$$

(a) calculate the values of

  (i) P(1)   (ii) P(2)   (iii) P(3)   (iv) P(4)

  (v) P(–1)   (vi) P(–2)   (vii) P(–3)   (viii) P(–4)

(b) write down three factors of P(x)

(c) confirm your answers to (b) by multiplying the three factors together.

2 The cubic polynomial P(x) is $x^3 - x^2 - 10x - 8$.

(a) To check whether $x + 2$ is a factor of P(x), for which value of a should you choose to calculate P(a)?

(b) Is $x + 2$ a factor of P(x)?

3 (a) If $P(x) = (x - 2)(x^2 - x - 2)$, explain why P(2) = 0.

(b) More generally, if $P(x) = (x - a)Q(x)$, where Q(x) is a polynomial, explain why P(a) = 0.

In question 3(b) you proved that:

> If $x - a$ is a factor of P(x), then P(a) = 0
>
> The converse, and more useful, result that
>
> If P(a) = 0, then $x - a$ is a factor of P(x)
>
> can also be shown to be true and is known as the **factor theorem.**

4 Use the factor theorem to factorise $x^3 - 3x^2 - x + 3$.

Often it is quite easy to spot one factor, but finding all three can be much harder. Questions 5 – 9 show how you can find the remaining factors without relying too much on inspiration!

5 Expand

(a) $(x - 3)(x^2 + 5x + 6)$

(b) $(x + 4)(x^2 + x - 2)$

6 If $x^3 - 19x + 30 = (x + 5)(x^2 - 5x + a)$, find a.

7 (a) Expand the polynomial P(x) if

$$P(x) = (x + 1)(x^2 - bx + 2)$$

(b) What is the value of b if

$$P(x) = x^3 - 2x^2 - x + 2$$

8 For each polynomial use the method of question 7 to find b and hence factorise the polynomial completely.

(a) $x^3 + x^2 - 5x + 3 = (x - 1)(x^2 + bx - 3)$

(b) $x^3 - 9x^2 + 6x + 56 = (x - 7)(x^2 + bx - 8)$

9 If $(x + 2)$ is a factor of P(x) = $x^3 - x^2 - 10x - 8$, then

$$x^3 - x^2 - 10x - 8 = (x + 2)\ (ax^2 + bx + c)$$

(a) (i) What is the value of a?

(ii) What is the value of c?

(b) Find b.

(c) Hence write P(x) as the product of three factors.

10 Use the factor theorem to find one factor, and then use the method of questions 6 – 9 to find the remaining factors of each of the following equations.

(a) $x^3 + 9x^2 + 2x - 48$

(b) $x^3 - 3x^2 + x - 3$

5 Numerical methods

5.1 The golden ratio

In chapter 4 you looked at techniques for solving polynomial equations. Although you found a formula that works for **all** quadratic equations, the method that you used for cubic and quartic equations will only work if the factors can be found easily. In fact there are general methods of solving both of these types of equation, but they are beyond the scope of this course.

In this chapter you will look at alternative ways of solving equations, using numerical techniques. These techniques do not give the **exact** solution to an equation, but will often give **good approximations** in cases where exact methods break down.

> How could you use a graph sketching package to solve
>
> $2^x = 5$

Tasksheet 1 introduces two important numerical techniques for solving equations.

T A S K S H E E T   1   –   The golden ratio (page 111)

5.2 Locating roots

The tasksheet described two numerical methods for solving an equation – a decimal search and an iterative process. Both methods had the same first step of approximately locating any solutions by plotting a graph.

Two possible arrangements of the equation from tasksheet 1 are

$$x^2 = x + 1 \text{ and } x^2 - x - 1 = 0$$

(a) In each arrangement

    (i) what graphs should you draw?

    (ii) which points give the solutions?

(b) Sketch the graphs and find bounds for the roots.

(c) Use the 'zoom' facility of a graph plotter to find the roots to 3 decimal places. Help is given on Technology datasheet: *Zoom*.

(d) What are the advantages and disadvantages of the two arrangements?

E X A M P L E   1

Find bounds for the solutions of

$$x^2 = 1 + \frac{1}{x + 3}.$$

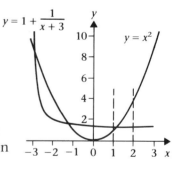

S O L U T I O N

From the graph, it can be seen that roots lie between -3 and -2, between -2 and -1 and between 1 and 2.

Graphs can be drawn very easily using a graph plotter, but care is needed to ensure that all the solutions are displayed on the screen.

E X E R C I S E   1

1 For each of the following, sketch appropriate graphs and find bounds for all the possible solutions

(a) $x^2 - 1 = 5\sqrt{x}$ (b) $x^3 + 3x^2 - 2x - 2 = 0$

(c) $2^x = 5 - x$ (d) $10 - x^2 = 2\,|\,x\,|$

2 Solve each equation correct to 2 decimal places.

5.3 Iterative formulas

One method of solving an equation is to use a 'zoom' facility on a graph plotter. An alternative method of reaching a solution was described in tasksheet 1. This iterative method consists of taking an initial value and using a formula to obtain a sequence of values which converges to the solution. Such formulas can be obtained by rearranging the equation into the form

$x = g(x)$

which suggests the iterative formula $x_{i+1} = g(x_i)$

EXAMPLE 2

Find the positive root of the equation $x^3 - 8x - 7 = 0$ correct to 3 decimal places.

SOLUTION

Step 1: Obtain the iterative formula.

$$x^3 - 8x - 7 = 0$$
$$\Rightarrow x^3 = 8x + 7$$
$$\Rightarrow x = \sqrt[3]{8x + 7}$$

which suggests the iterative formula

$$x_{i+1} = \sqrt[3]{8x_i + 7}$$

Step 2: Sketch the graph to locate the roots.

Step 3: From the graph, choose a suitable value for x_1.

$x_1 = 3$ is nearest to the solution.

Step 4: Use the formula to generate the iterative sequence.

$$x_2 = \sqrt[3]{8 \times 3 + 7} = 3.141380652$$

$$x_3 = 3.179129979$$

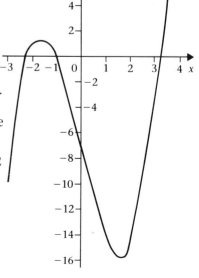

(a) Find x_4.

(b) Continue to find x_5, x_6, x_7 etc. until you are confident that you know the solution to 3 decimal places. How can you decide when to stop?

(c) In writing out your solutions, how many decimal places is it sensible to give for your intermediate results?

Help in generating iterative sequences is given on Technology datasheet: *Repeated calculations.*

T A S K S H E E T 2 – *Iterative formulas (page 118)*

E X E R C I S E 2

1 For the equation $x^3 = 10$

(a) (i) show that the equation can be arranged into the form $x = \sqrt{\dfrac{10}{x}}$

(ii) by letting $x_1 = 2$, and using an iterative formula, obtain the positive solution for $x^3 = 10$ to 5 decimal places;

(b) (i) show that the equation can be rearranged to $x = \sqrt{\sqrt{10x}}$;

(ii) by letting $x_1 = 2$ and using an iterative formula, obtain the positive solution for $x^3 = 10$ to 5 decimal places.

2 Using an initial value of $x_1 = 3$ and an iterative formula, find a positive solution of $2^x = 3x$ to 4 decimal places.

3 (a) By sketching appropriate graphs, find an interval that contains the root of

$$x^2 - 1 = 6\sqrt{x}$$

(b) Show that $x = \sqrt{6\sqrt{x} + 1}$ is a rearrangement of this equation.

(c) By choosing an appropriate starting value, solve the equation giving your answer correct to 6 decimal places.

4 (a) Show that the equation $x^3 + 2x = 1$ has a root that lies between 0 and 1.

(b) Show that $x = \dfrac{(1 - x^3)}{2}$ is a rearrangement of the equation.

(c) Find the root between 0 and 1 correct to 5 decimal places using a starting value of (i) 0 (ii) 1.

(d) What happens if you take a starting value of 2?

5 This question concerns the equation $2x^2 - 5x + 1 = 0$ and three of the possible rearrangements which were considered on tasksheet 2. All answers should be given to 6 decimal places.

(a) Show that the equation $2x^2 - 5x + 1 = 0$ has one root in the interval $[0,1]$ and another in the interval $[2,3]$.

(b) For the iterative formula $x_{i+1} = \sqrt{\dfrac{5x_i - 1}{2}}$:

(i) explain why the starting value $x_1 = 0$ cannot be used;

(ii) solve the equation using starting values of 1, 2 and 10. Record the number of iterations used for each starting value.

(c) Solve the equation using the iterative formula

$$x_{i+1} = \frac{1}{2}\left(5 - \frac{1}{x_i}\right)$$

and starting values (i) 1   (ii) 2   (iii) 10.

Record the number of iterations used for each starting value.

(d) Solve the equation using the iterative formula

$$x_{i+1} = \frac{1 + 2x_i^2}{5}$$

and starting values   (i) 1

(ii) 2

(iii) 3.

(e) Comment on the suitability of each formula.

5.4 Convergence (extension section)

In the previous section you solved the equation $2x^2 - 5x + 1 = 0$ using a variety of formulas and starting points, of which some converged rapidly, some converged more slowly, some converged to a root in a different interval and some did not converge at all!

Clearly the choice of an iterative formula is critical if you are to obtain a sequence which converges quickly.

In order to see what is happening, it is interesting to view the process diagrammatically.

TASKSHEET 3E – Convergence of iterative sequences (page 119)

EXAMPLE 3

Illustrate the convergence of the iterative formula

$$x_{i+1} = \sqrt{\frac{10}{x_i}}$$

with starting value $x_1 = 2$ using a cobweb diagram.

SOLUTION

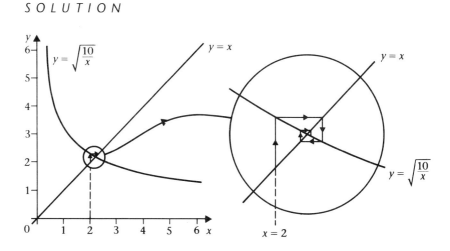

Convergence occurs here because, near the root, the graph is sufficiently flat.

The convergence of iterative sequences is of interest in various areas of mathematics. For example, the iterative process based upon the sequence $x_{i+1} = \lambda x_i (1 - x_i)$ is at the heart of the recently developed mathematical theory of **chaos**.

After working through this chapter you should:

1 know how to solve equations approximately by drawing graphs;

2 be able to obtain bounds for solutions of $f(x) = 0$ by looking for changes of sign of $f(x)$;

3 be able to use the iterative formula $x_{i+1} = g(x_i)$ to obtain a root to a given degree of accuracy;

4 be able to rearrange equations into the form $x = g(x)$;

5 appreciate that the iterative method based upon $x = g(x)$ may or may not converge.

The golden ratio

Given a square, can a rectangle be 'added'

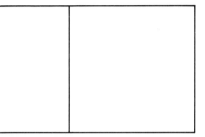

so that the shape of the new rectangle is the same as that of the added rectangle, as shown below?

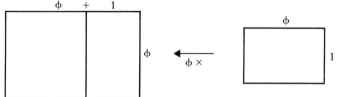

A rectangle with this shape is called a **golden rectangle** and the ratio of the lengths of its sides is called the **golden ratio**. Later you will see that there is only one possible value for this ratio. It is denoted by the Greek symbol ϕ (phi) in honour of the great sculptor Phidias who used it in his work. Like other famous mathematical constants such as π and e, ϕ is found in many situations. Many mythical and mystical properties were attributed to ϕ, which may explain the use of the term 'golden'.

How can you find the golden ratio? Comparing the added rectangle with the new rectangle,

you can see that the ratio of the shorter sides is ϕ. The ratio of the longer sides must also be ϕ and so

$$\phi \times \phi = \phi + 1$$

> **1** Explain why $\phi \times \phi = \phi + 1$.

ϕ therefore satisfies the quadratic equation

$$x^2 = x + 1$$

or, rearranging, $x^2 - x - 1 = 0$.

This equation can of course be solved using the formula, but in this instance you are going to see how it can be solved numerically.

If you put $x^2 - x - 1$ into the completed

square form, $\left(x - \dfrac{1}{2} \right)^2 - \dfrac{5}{4}$ the graph is

easy to sketch.

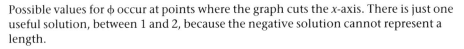

Possible values for ϕ occur at points where the graph cuts the x-axis. There is just one useful solution, between 1 and 2, because the negative solution cannot represent a length.

Now that you know an approximate value of ϕ you can find it more precisely by using the method of **decimal search**.

Begin the decimal search by considering values of x between 1 and 2 in steps of 0.1.

x	$x^2 - x - 1$
1.0	−1
1.1	−0.89
1.2	−0.76
1.3	−0.61
1.4	−0.44
1.5	−0.25
1.6	−0.04 } solution
1.7	0.19 } here
1.8	0.44
1.9	0.71
2.0	1

2 How do you know there is a solution between 1.6 and 1.7?

The search continues between 1.6 and 1.7 in steps of 0.01

x	$x^2 - x - 1$	
1.60	-0.04	
1.61	-0.0179	solution
1.62	0.0044	here
1.63	0.0269	
–	–	
–	–	

After two searches, it can be seen that the solution lies between 1.61 and 1.62, hence the solution is 1.6 (to 1 d.p.). Further searches would increase the accuracy by one decimal place at a time.

> **3**   Can you suggest how to speed up the method of decimal search?

The cold facts discussed so far have not done justice to the history of the golden ratio, from the serious school of Pythagoras to the fanciful theories of enthusiasts. Perhaps the most important work was done by Leonardo of Pisa (b.1175) otherwise known as Fibonacci. His study of natural phenomena led to the sequence of numbers which bears his name:

1 1 2 3 5 8 13 21 34 55 . . .

which can be defined inductively by

$u_1 = 1, u_2 = 1,$
$u_i = u_{i-1} + u_{i-2}$, for $i \geq 3$.

Numbers from this sequence arise in many surprising contexts, including the structure of a beehive, the population of a rabbit warren and the white and black notes on a piano keyboard. Many plants have spiral patterns of petals or leaves and the number of spirals is invariably a number from the Fibonacci sequence. A detailed study shows that the sunflower head has 21 spirals in the clockwise direction and 34 in the anticlockwise, whilst the pine cone has 8 clockwise and 13 anticlockwise parts.

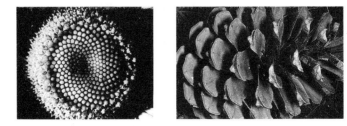

Another major contribution Fibonacci made to mathematics was his promotion of the Arabic system of numbers, which we use today.

What is the connection between the golden ratio and Fibonacci numbers?

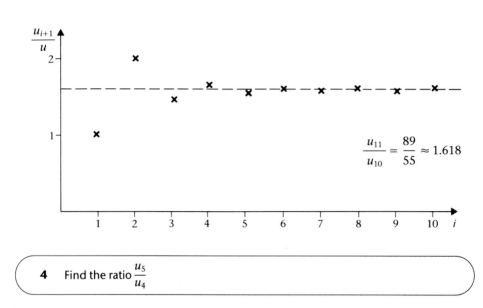

$$\frac{u_{11}}{u_{10}} = \frac{89}{55} \approx 1.618$$

4　Find the ratio $\dfrac{u_5}{u_4}$

This sequence coverges to the golden ratio, ϕ, i.e.

$$\frac{u_i}{u_{i-1}} \to \phi \qquad \text{as } i \to \infty$$

There is a fascinating visual connection between the Fibonacci sequence and the golden ratio via the golden rectangle.

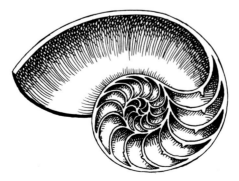

As the shell of the chambered nautilus grows, the size of the chambers increases but their shape remains unchanged.

The same spiral shape can be constructed using golden rectangles.

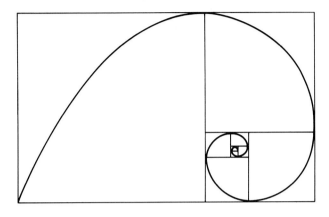

The convergence of the sequence of ratios suggests that an iterative method of solution could be used to evaluate the golden ratio. For such an approach, you need a recurrence relation or iterative formula to set up a sequence of values.

The equation $x^2 = x + 1$ can be written as $x = \sqrt{x + 1}$. (The root given by $x = -\sqrt{x + 1}$ is rejected as you are only interested in the positive root.)

If the sequence generated by the formula

$$x_{i+1} = \sqrt{x_i + 1}$$

converged, then the limiting value x would satisfy $x = \sqrt{x + 1}$ and would therefore satisfy $x^2 = x + 1$.

From the sketch of the graph, $x_1 = 1$ seems an appropriate choice for the first term of the sequence. Then

$x_2 = 1.4142136$	$x_8 = 1.6178513$
$x_3 = 1.5537740$	$x_9 = 1.6179775$
$x_4 = 1.5980532$	$x_{10} = 1.6180165$
$x_5 = 1.6118478$	$x_{11} = 1.6180286$
$x_6 = 1.6161212$	$x_{12} = 1.6180323.$
$x_7 = 1.6174428$	

> **5** Explain how the value of x_2 is obtained.

This sequence clearly converges to a solution for x which is 1.618 (to 3 d.p.) Using an 8-digit display calculator, the value 1.6180340 is obtained after sixteen iterations and remains unchanged by any further iterations.

As well as fascinating mathematics, the 'golden' property has also attracted the attention of philosophers, architects and artists over the centuries.

It has been claimed that the golden rectangle

$\phi \approx 1.618$

is *the* most artistically pleasing rectangle.

An attempt at confirming or denying this was made by Gustav Fechner in 1876. His extensive experiments did confirm that the most aesthetically pleasing shape for a rectangle was something between that of a square and a rectangle with sides in the ratio 1 : 2.

Architecturally, some very famous and beautiful structures, for example the Parthenon, are said to be based on the golden ratio and rectangle.

Finally, it would be satisfying if an exact representation of the 'golden' number could be given. For this it is necessary to use the quadratic formula for the solution of $x^2 - x - 1 = 0$.

$$x = \frac{1 \pm \sqrt{1 + 4}}{2}$$

$$= \frac{1}{2} + \frac{1}{2}\sqrt{5} \text{ or } \frac{1}{2} - \frac{1}{2}\sqrt{5}$$

$\sqrt{5}$ is a number written in **surd** form. This means that the square root sign remains, rather than replacing $\sqrt{5}$ with its decimal value of 2.236068 (to 7 s.f.) which would be clumsy to write out every time, and which of course has a small error associated with it.

---

6   How big is this error?

As seen earlier the negative value is discarded, so

The golden ratio is

$$\phi = \frac{1}{2}(1 + \sqrt{5})$$

$$\phi \approx 1.618034$$

If you would like to find out more about the golden ratio, many recreational mathematics books have chapters devoted to it. A very readable book is:

H. E. Huntley, *The Divine Proportion*, Dover, 1970.

Iterative formulas

One type of iterative formula can be obtained by rearranging an equation into the form

$$x = g(x)$$

which may then be written as the iterative formula

$$x_{i+1} = g(x_i)$$

For example, to show that $x^2 - 3x + 2 = 0$ can be rearranged into the iterative formula

$$x_{i+1} = \frac{x_i^2 + 2}{3}$$

proceed as follows:

$$x^2 - 3x + 2 = 0 \quad \Rightarrow \quad x^2 + 2 = 3x \quad \Rightarrow \quad x = \frac{x^2 + 2}{3}$$

$$\Rightarrow \quad x_{i+1} = \frac{x_i^2 + 2}{3}$$

Alternatively, since the steps are reversible, it is sometimes easier to work backwards,

i.e. $\qquad x = \dfrac{x^2 + 2}{3}$

$$\Rightarrow \qquad 3x = x^2 + 2$$

$$\Rightarrow x^2 - 3x + 2 = 0.$$

1 For the equation

$$2x^2 - 5x + 1 = 0$$

find which of the following are possible iterative formulas and show how they can be obtained.

(a) $x_{i+1} = \sqrt{\dfrac{5x_i - 1}{2}}$

(b) $x_{i+1} = \dfrac{1 + 2x_i^2}{5}$

(c) $x_{i+1} = \dfrac{1}{2}\left(5 - \dfrac{1}{x_i}\right)$

(d) $x_{i+1} = \dfrac{1}{5 - 2x_i}$

(e) $x_{i+1} = \dfrac{1}{2}\sqrt{1 - 5x_i}$

(f) $x_{i+1} = 2x_i^2 - 4x_i + 1$

(g) $x_{i+1} = 1 + \dfrac{1}{2}\sqrt{x_i + 1}$

(h) $x_{i+1} = -\dfrac{1}{5}(1 - 2x_i^2)$

(i) $x_{i+1} = \sqrt{5x_i - 1 - x_i^2}$

(j) $x_{i+1} = 2 + \sqrt{\dfrac{7 - 3x_i}{2}}$

Convergence of iterative sequences

1 (a) Give a rough estimate for $\sqrt[3]{10}$.

(b) Explain how the rearrangement $x = \dfrac{10}{x^2}$

is obtained from $x^3 = 10$.

Use the iterative formula $x_{i+1} = \dfrac{10}{x_i^{\,2}}$, together with the starting value that

you gave in part (a), to evaluate $x_2, x_3, \ldots, x_{10}$. What do you find?

It is helpful to know when a sequence is likely to converge *before* working out all the values. This tasksheet shows how a graphical approach can help to predict convergence.

2 Consider the rearranged equation $x = \dfrac{10}{x^2}$.

This is equivalent to the two simultaneous equations

$$y = x \ \text{ and } \ y = \frac{10}{x^2}$$

and its solution lies at the intersection of the two graphs.

(a) For $0 \le x \le 3$, plot $y = x$ and $y = \dfrac{10}{x^2}$ on the same graph. You can now

illustrate the solution procedure for a particular starting value, say $x_1 = 2$.

$$x_1 = 2 \Rightarrow g(x_1) = \frac{10}{2^2} = 2.5. \text{ Therefore } x_2 = 2.5$$

(b) On your graph, plot and join the points (x_1, x_1), (x_1, x_2) and (x_2, x_2) as shown above. How could you have used your graph to locate the points (x_1, x_2) and (x_2, x_2) *without* doing any calculations?

(c) *Without* further calculation, plot and successively join up the points (x_2, x_3), (x_3, x_3), (x_3, x_4), (x_4, x_4).

The diagram you have obtained should be a **cobweb** diagram.

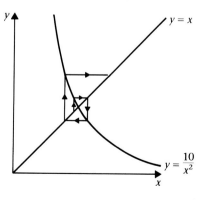

3 What does the cobweb diagram of question 2 illustrate about the iteration attempted in question 1?

4 (a) Draw a cobweb diagram for the function $g(x)$ illustrated. (It is not necessary to give $g(x)$ an equation – simply use the construction described in question 2.)

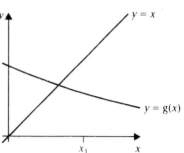

(b) What would happen in this case to the sequence defined by $x_{i+1} = g(x_i)$?

5 Draw similar diagrams for the following functions and describe their behaviour.

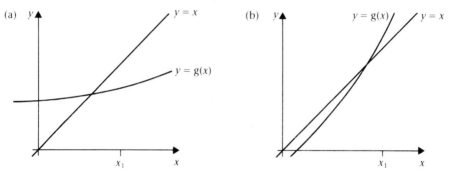

(a)

(b)

What happens in each case if x_1 is on the other side of the root?

6 In question 5, **staircase** diagrams should have been obtained. What property of $g(x)$ determines whether or not you get a staircase or a cobweb diagram?

7 By considering the staircase and cobweb diagrams above, explain how the gradient of $g(x)$ determines whether an iteration based upon

$$x_{i+1} = g(x_i)$$

will converge or diverge.

8 For $x^3 = 10$

(a) show how to obtain the iterative formula

$$x_{i+1} = \frac{1}{3}\left(2x_i + \frac{10}{x_i^2}\right)$$

(b) using appropriate staircase or cobweb diagrams, investigate the convergence of the iterative sequence obtained for different initial values.

Solutions

1 Graphs

1.1 Introduction

(a) Use the graph to copy and complete this table.

(b) Draw a graph from this table, plotting total profit against profit per radio. (The solution to the trader's problem should now be quite easy to see.)

(c) What profit per radio should she choose?

(a)

Profit (£) per radio	0	1	2	3	4	5	6
Number of radios sold	60	50	40	30	20	10	0
Total profit (£) from sales	0	50	80	90	80	50	0

(b) When the phrase 'plotting _ _ _ _ _ against _ _ _ _ _' is used then:

this quantity is assigned to the horizontal axis.

this quantity is assigned to the vertical axis.

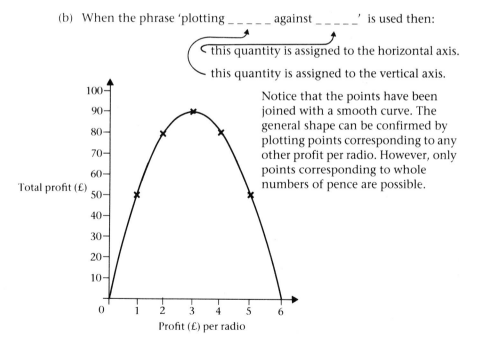

Notice that the points have been joined with a smooth curve. The general shape can be confirmed by plotting points corresponding to any other profit per radio. However, only points corresponding to whole numbers of pence are possible.

(c) The maximum total profit is £90, which is obtained with a profit per radio of £3.

1.2 Linear functions

> (a) What distance has the walker covered after one day and how far is he from Land's End?
>
> (b) How far has he walked after two days and how far is he from Land's End?
>
> (c) How far has he walked after t days and how far is he from Land's End?
>
> (d) What are the equations of the two graphs of distance against time?

	No. of days	Distance walked (miles)	Distance from Land's End (miles)
(a)	1	30	770
(b)	2	60	740
(c)	t	$30t$	$800 - 30t$

(d) In the first graph, s represents the distance, in miles, walked from John O'Groats, which is $30t$. Therefore, $s = 30t$ is the equation of the graph.

In the second graph, s represents the distance, in miles, from Land's End, which is $800 - 30t$. Therefore, $s = 800 - 30t$ is the equation of the graph.

> How would you find the equation of the straight line through $(1, 2)$ and $(3, 8)$?

You may have used a graphical method or perhaps you used the equation $y = mx + c$, as shown below:

$$m = \frac{8 - 2}{3 - 1} = 3 \quad \text{(gradient)}$$
$$\Rightarrow y = 3x + c \quad (\Rightarrow \text{means 'implies')}$$

$(1, 2)$ is a point on the line.

So $2 = 3 \times 1 + c$

$$\Rightarrow c = -1$$

So the equation is $y = 3x - 1$.

(a) Do different methods give the same equation?

(b) Show that using $\dfrac{y-8}{x-3}$ as the gradient gives the same equation.

(a) Yes, but the equations may be in different forms. For example, $y - 2 = 3(x - 1)$ is the same equation as $y = 3x - 1$ because

$$y - 2 = 3(x - 1)$$

$$\Rightarrow y - 2 = 3x - 3$$

$$\Rightarrow \quad y = 3x - 1$$

(b) $\dfrac{y-8}{x-3} = \dfrac{6}{2} = 3$

$$\Rightarrow y - 8 = 3(x - 3)$$

$$\Rightarrow \quad y = 3x - 1$$

E X E R C I S E 1

1 (a)

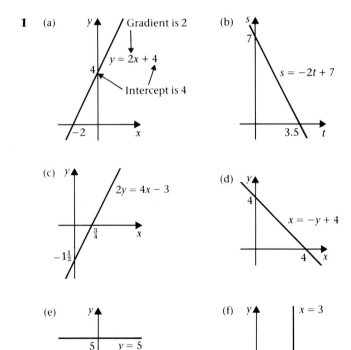

(a) Gradient is 2, $y = 2x + 4$, Intercept is 4, -2, 4

(b) $s = -2t + 7$, 7, 3.5

(c) $2y = 4x - 3$, $\frac{3}{4}$, $-1\frac{1}{2}$

(d) $x = -y + 4$, 4, 4

(e) $y = 5$, 5

(f) $x = 3$, 3

2 (a) $y = 2x + 2$ (b) $y = -2x + 4$

(c) $s = \frac{1}{2}t + 3$ or $2s = t + 6$ (d) $y = \frac{3}{2}x - 2$ or $2y = 3x - 4$

3 (a) $y = 2x + 3$

(b) $\dfrac{y - 6}{x - 2} = 2$ ① or $\dfrac{y - 4}{x - 1} = 2$ ②

       $\Rightarrow y = 2x + 2$ $\Rightarrow y = 2x + 2$

The equations ① and ② are acceptable equations of a straight line; the rearrangement has been given to show that they are equivalent.

(c) $\dfrac{y - 0}{x + 4} = \dfrac{5}{-5}$ $\Rightarrow y = -x - 4$

(d) $\dfrac{y - 2}{x - 1} = \dfrac{1}{3}$ or $\dfrac{y - 1}{x + 2} = \dfrac{1}{3}$

Both give $3y = x + 5$.

4 (a) No   (b) yes, gradient $-\frac{1}{2}$, intercept 2

(c) no   (d) no

(e) yes, gradient $-\frac{1}{2}$, intercept $\frac{5}{2}$ (f) yes, parallel to the y-axis

(g) yes, gradient 4, intercept 7   (h) yes, gradient $-\frac{3}{2}$, intercept 3

(i) no

An equation will *only* have a straight-line graph if it can be written in the form $y = mx + c$.

1.4   Completing the square

EXERCISE 2

1 (a) (i) $(x + 4)^2 - 11$ (iii)

         (ii) $x^2 + 8x + 16 - 11$

            $= x^2 + 8x + 5$

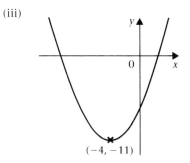

$(-4, -11)$

(b) (i) $(x - 2)^2 - 7$ (iii)

(ii) $x^2 - 4x + 4 - 7$

$= x^2 - 4x - 3$

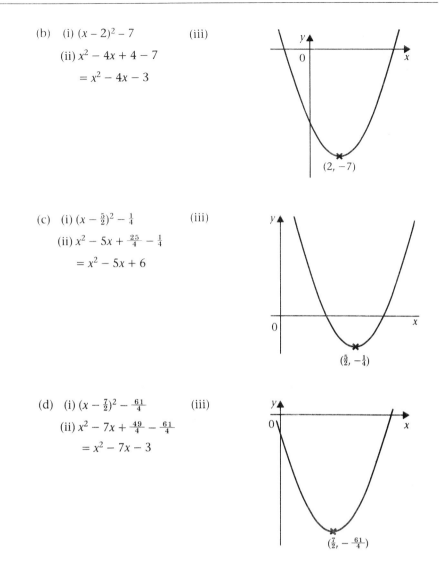

(2, −7)

(c) (i) $(x - \frac{5}{2})^2 - \frac{1}{4}$ (iii)

(ii) $x^2 - 5x + \frac{25}{4} - \frac{1}{4}$

$= x^2 - 5x + 6$

$(\frac{5}{2}, -\frac{1}{4})$

(d) (i) $(x - \frac{7}{2})^2 - \frac{61}{4}$ (iii)

(ii) $x^2 - 7x + \frac{49}{4} - \frac{61}{4}$

$= x^2 - 7x - 3$

$(\frac{7}{2}, -\frac{61}{4})$

2 (a) (i) $y = (x + 2)^2 + 3$ (ii) $y = (x - 2)^2 - 5$

(b) (i) $y = x^2 + 4x + 7$ (ii) $y = x^2 - 4x + 4 - 5 \Rightarrow y = x^2 - 4x - 1$

125

1.6 Factorising quadratics

EXERCISE 3

1 (a) $(x + 3)(x + 4)$ (b) $(x - 3)(x + 1)$ (c) $(x - 5)(x - 2)$

   (d) $(x + 2)(x - 2)$ (e) $x(x - 7)$ (f) $(x - 3)^2$

   (g) $(x + 1)(x + 2)$ (h) $(x + 2)^2$ (i) $(x + 7)(x - 7)$

2 (a)

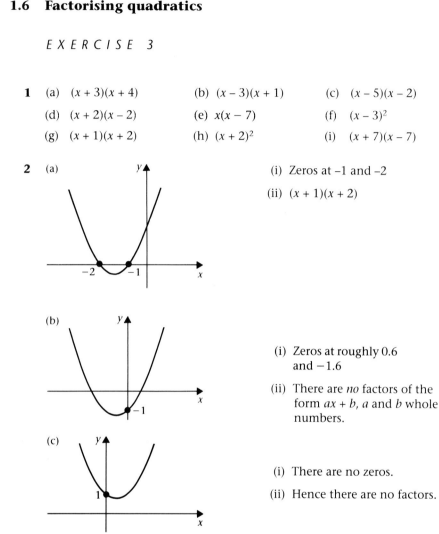

(i) Zeros at -1 and -2

(ii) $(x + 1)(x + 2)$

(b)

(i) Zeros at roughly 0.6 and -1.6

(ii) There are *no* factors of the form $ax + b$, a and b whole numbers.

(c)

(i) There are no zeros.

(ii) Hence there are no factors.

2 Sequences

2.1 Sequences in action

> What would be a sensible prediction for the population in 1995?

The population would be $180.14 \times 1.024 = 184.46$ million.

2.2 Generating sequences

EXERCISE 1

1 $u_1 = 4$, $u_2 = 8$, $u_3 = 16$, $u_4 = 32$, $u_5 = 64$. The sequence is diverging.

2 (a) $u_1 = 9$, $u_2 = 6$, $u_3 = 4$, $u_4 = \frac{8}{3}$; converging

   (b) $u_1 = 2$, $u_2 = \frac{1}{4}$, $u_3 = 16$; diverging

   (c) $u_1 = 1$, $u_2 = 5$, $u_3 = 1$, $u_4 = 5$; oscillating

3 $u_1 = 1$, $u_2 = 1\frac{1}{2}$, $u_3 = 1\frac{3}{4}$, $u_4 = 1\frac{7}{8}$, $u_5 = 1\frac{15}{16}$

   The sequence is converging, approaching the limit of 2.

4 The sequence is 1, 2, 3, 5, 8, 13, 21, 34, . . ., which diverges.

5 The sequence is 2, 6.75, 0.5926, 76.88, 0.0046, 1 294 319.3, . . .

   Odd terms approach zero, whilst the remaining terms become very large.

6 (a) $u_1 = 1$, $u_{i+1} = \frac{1}{2}u_i$ (b) $u_i = 1$, $u_{i+1} = \left(-\frac{1}{2}\right)u_i$

2.3 The general term

> (a) What is s_{50}?   (b) What is s_t?
>
> (c) Why is it inappropriate to use an inductive method to calculate s_{50}?

(a) $s_{50} = 300$ (b) $s_t = 6t$

(c) The inductive method requires every term in turn to be calculated, in this case a further forty-nine terms!

2.4 Arithmetic series

EXERCISE 2

1 (a) $\left(\dfrac{4 + 199}{2}\right) \times 40 = 4060$ (b) $\dfrac{50}{2}(6 + 49 \times 6) = 7500$

  (c) $\left(\dfrac{1 + 100}{2}\right) \times 199 = 10049\frac{1}{2}$ (d) $\left(\dfrac{99 + 25}{2}\right) \times 38 = 2356$

2 (a) Last term $= 8 + 17 \times 2 = 42;$ sum $= \left(\dfrac{8 + 42}{2}\right) \times 18 = 450$

  (b) number of terms $= \dfrac{303 - 6}{9} + 1 = 34;$ sum $= \left(\dfrac{6 + 303}{2}\right) \times 34 = 5253$

  (c) common difference $= \dfrac{195 - 3}{24} = 8;$ sum $= \left(\dfrac{3 + 195}{2}\right) \times 25 = 2475$

3 The volume under the bottom step is

$$V = 50 \times \frac{1}{4} \times \frac{3}{4} \, \text{m}^3$$

Successive steps up have volumes $2V, 3V, \ldots, 15V$.

The total volume is therefore

$$15 \times \frac{V + 15V}{2} = 120V \, \text{m} = 1125 \, \text{m}^3$$

2.5 Finance

> If Jo's savings at the start of year k are £S_k, explain why her savings a year later, £S_{k+1}, are given by
>
> $S_{k+1} = S_k \times 1.08 + 1000$

At an interest rate of 8 per cent, the amount invested, £S_k, is increased by a factor of

$$\frac{108}{100} = 1.08$$

to £$1.08\,S_k$.

If a further £1000 is invested the following January, her total investment at the start of year $k + 1$ is

$$£(S_k \times 1.08 + 1000)$$

2.6 Sigma notation

> Why can the 1000 be taken outside the summation?

1000 is a **common factor** of each term of the series

$$1000 \times 1.08 + 1000 \times 1.08^2 + \ldots + 1000 \times 1.08^{10}$$

The series can therefore be factorised as

$$1000 \times (1.08 + 1.08^2 + \ldots + 1.08^{10})$$

$$= 1000 \sum_{i=1}^{10} 1.08^i$$

> Is this the only way of expressing this series?

No. You could, for example, write the general term as $2i + 1$, where i goes from 1 to 49, which would give

$$\sum_{i=1}^{49} (2i + 1)$$

Alternatively, you could write it as $\displaystyle\sum_{i=2}^{50} (2i - 1)$, or in many other ways!

E X E R C I S E 3

1 (a) $1 + \frac{1}{2} + \frac{1}{3} + \frac{1}{4} + \frac{1}{5}$ (b) $9 + 16 + 25 + 36 + 49$

(c) $\frac{1}{2} + \frac{1}{6} + \frac{1}{12} + \frac{1}{20} + \frac{1}{30}$ (d) $11 - 13 + 15 - 17 + 19$

(e) $1 + 8 + 27 + 64 + 125 + 216$ (f) $1 + 8 + 27 + 64 + 125 + 216$

Note that (e) and (f) are different representations of the same sum.

2 (a) $\displaystyle\sum_{i=1}^{50} \sqrt{i}$ (b) $\displaystyle\sum_{i=1}^{50} (2i)^2$ (c) $\displaystyle\sum_{i=1}^{49} \frac{1}{2i+1}$

(d) $\displaystyle\sum_{i=1}^{19} (-1)^{i+1} i^3$ (e) $\displaystyle\sum_{i=1}^{99} \frac{i}{i+1}$

3 (a) $7 + 10 + \ldots + 64$ (20 terms) (b) $35 + 33 + \ldots + (-3)$ (20 terms)

$$= 20 \times \frac{7 + 64}{2}$$ $$= 20 \times \frac{35 - 3}{2}$$

$$= 710$$ $$= 320$$

2.7 Geometric series

EXERCISE 4

1 (a) $\dfrac{2\,(3^8 - 1)}{2} = 6560$ (b) $122\,070\,312$ (c) $1\,743\,392\,200$

   (d) $15.984\,375$ (e) $5.328\,125$

2 (a) $1 + 3 + 9 + 27 + 81 = 121$

   (b) $1 + 8 + 8^2 + \ldots + 8^9 = 153\,391\,689 \approx 1.53 \times 10^8$, which is more practical expression.

   (c) $2 + 2^2 + \ldots + 2^7 = 2 \left(\dfrac{2^7 - 1}{2 - 1} \right) = 254$

   (d) $\left(\dfrac{1}{2}\right)^3 \left[1 + \dfrac{1}{2} + \ldots + \left(\dfrac{1}{2}\right)^5 \right] = \dfrac{63}{256}$ (e) $\dfrac{1 - (-\frac{3}{4})^{20}}{1 - (-\frac{3}{4})} = 0.570$ (to 3 s.r.)

3 (a) He requested $1 + 2 + 4 + 8 + \ldots + 2^{63} = \dfrac{2^{64} - 1}{2 - 1} \approx 1.84 \times 10^{19}$ grains!

   (b) 3.7×10^{17}g or 3.7×10^{11} tonnes!

4 (a) The value increases by a factor of 1.01 per annum. After 2090 years it would be worth $1 \times 1.01^{2090} = 1\,075\,650\,5\,55$p or approximately £10.8 million.

   (b) Replacing 1.01 by 1.05 in (a) gives £1.9×10^{42}!

5 $\dfrac{200 \times 1.05\,(1.05^{50} - 1)}{1.05 - 1} = £43\,963$ (to the nearest pound).

6   Taking the school leaver's salary as £8000, the total earnings over a 45 year period would be

$$£8000\,(1 + 1.1 + 1.1^2 + \ldots + 1.1^{44}) = £8000\,\dfrac{(1.1^{45} - 1)}{1.1 - 1} \approx £5.75 \text{ million}$$

7 (a) $\dfrac{1000 \times 1.075\,(1.075^n - 1)}{1.075 - 1}$

   (b) The conditions lead to the equation

$$\dfrac{1000 \times 1.075\,(1.075^n - 1)}{1.075 - 1} = 2000n$$

   The conditions are met after 17 years.

2.8 Infinity

E X E R C I S E 5

1 (a) $\dfrac{\frac{9}{10}}{1 - \frac{1}{10}} = 1$ (b) $\dfrac{4}{1 + \frac{3}{4}} = \dfrac{16}{7}$ (c) The sum diverges (d) $\dfrac{5}{1 - \frac{1}{2}} = 10$

2 (a) $\dfrac{3}{2}$ (b) $\dfrac{4}{3}$ (c) 1

3 (a) The sum is $\dfrac{1}{3}$.

(b) If you consider the diagram to be made up from a sequence of nested L shapes,

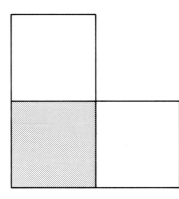 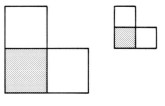

it can be seen that each L shape is made up of one shaded and two unshaded squares, i.e. $\frac{1}{3}$ of the diagram is shaded.

4 (a) 3 (b) 4 (c) $\dfrac{16}{3}$ (d) $3 \times \left(\dfrac{4}{3}\right)^{n}$

$\dfrac{4}{3} > 1$ therefore $\left(\dfrac{4}{3}\right)^{n} \to \infty$ as $n \to \infty$. This means $P_{n} \to \infty$ as $n \to \infty$.

The limiting curve is of infinite length, yet encloses a finite area!

5 The sum to n terms is

$$\dfrac{2(1 - (\frac{2}{5})^{n})}{1 - \frac{2}{5}} = \dfrac{10}{3}\left(1 - \left(\dfrac{2}{5}\right)^{n}\right).$$

The sum to infinity is $\dfrac{10}{3}$.

The difference, $\dfrac{10}{3}\left(\dfrac{2}{5}\right)^{n}$, is less than 0.01 when $n = 7$.

3 Functions and graphs

3.1 Function notation

E X E R C I S E   1

1 (a) 3   (b) 4   (c) 5   (d) 4

2 (a) $\dfrac{5}{9}$ (b) $\dfrac{5}{3}$ (c) 5   (d) 15   (e) $\dfrac{5}{3^x}$

3 (a) (i) 6   (ii) 0   (iii) 2   (iv) 0   (v) $n^2 + 3n + 2$

   (b) (i) 6   (ii) 0   (iii) 2   (iv) 0   (v) $n^2 + 3n + 2$

   (c) No, except that a different symbol is used for the variable.

3.3 Defining functions

> Use the new notation to define h, where $h(x) = \sqrt{x}, x \geq 0$.

$h(x) = \sqrt{x}, x \in \mathbb{R}^+$

E X E R C I S E   2

1 (a) (i) $\dfrac{1}{2}$ (ii) 1   (iii) $\dfrac{1}{a+2}$ (iv) $\dfrac{1}{a}$

   (v) $f(-2)$ is undefined.

   (b) All values of x, except $x = -2$

   (c)

2 (a) (i) $\sqrt{2}$ (ii) 3   (iii) $\sqrt[4]{2}$ (iv) $\sqrt{\pi}$ (v) π

   (b) $x \geq 0$ or $x \in \mathbb{R}$

   (c)

3 (a) All values of x, except $x = -5$

(b) $x > 3$; note that $x \neq 3$ because division by zero is undefined

(c) All values of x

(d) All values of x, except $x = -2$

4 (a) (i) 5   (ii) 7   (iii) $\sqrt{2}$ (iv) π (v) 0

(b) $\mathbb{R}$

(c)

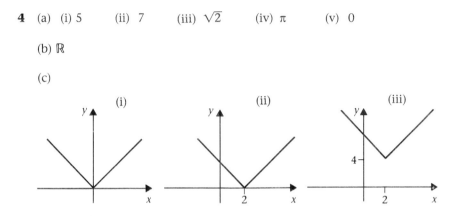

3.5 Features of graphs

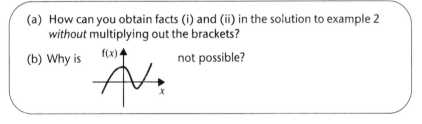

(a) How can you obtain facts (i) and (ii) in the solution to example 2 *without* multiplying out the brackets?

(b) Why is [graph] not possible?

(a) The relevant terms from each bracket are multiplied

$$f(0) = (-2)^2 \times 7 = 28 \quad \text{and} \quad x^2 \times (2x) = 2x^3.$$

(b) From the factorised form for $f(x)$, the graph can only cross (or touch) the x-axis at $-3\frac{1}{2}$ and 2.

Two other ideas connected with roots can be helpful in considering graphs:

(i) Find the sign of $f(x)$ between the roots.

x	-4	0	3
$f(x)$	-36	28	13
Sign of $f(x)$	$-$ve	$+$ve	$+$ve

The curve therefore crosses the x-axis at $-3\frac{1}{2}$ but touches it at $x = 2$.

(ii) When a factor is repeated twice, as in $(x - 2)^2$, you can imagine there to be *two* roots very close together at $x = 2$.

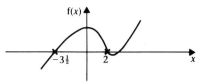

If you consider the two roots to merge together you obtain the required shape for the graph of $f(x)$.

E X E R C I S E   3

1 The zeros are at $-3, 2, \frac{7}{3}$. The dominant parts of the graph are indicated by the line segments. The dashes indicate the completed sketch.

2 The zeros are at $-\frac{2}{5}, 1, 4$ and the graph is:

3 $x^3(x +4)(x - 7) = x^5 - 3x^4 - 28x^3$

x^5 dominates for large x.
$-28x^3$ dominates for very small x.

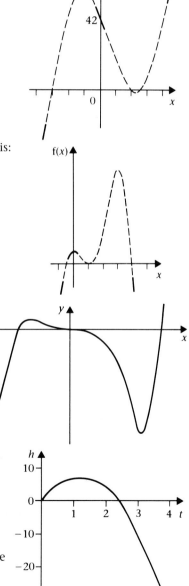

4 (a) The stone is level with the point of release when h is zero. This occurs when $t = 0$ or 2.4, and the relevant answer is 2.4 seconds.

(b) When $t = 4$ then $h = -32$. The point of release is 32 m above sea level and the height of the cliff will be a little less than this.

4 Expressions and equations

4.1 The language of algebra

(a) In the expression

$$y = ax^2 + bx + c$$

x is called the **independent** variable and y is called the **dependent** variable. What is meant by this?

(b) The letters a and x are both in the formula for y. In what way do they play different roles?

(a) y is given as a function of x and so y is considered to **depend** on x. Mathematically, the way an equation is written can alter which variable is considered to be dependent upon the other. However, the context can affect this decision. For example, if a is your age in year y, then it is natural to consider a to be dependent upon y, no matter whether the relationship is written as $y = a + 1976$ or $a = y - 1976$.

(b) $ax^2 + bx + c$ is usually considered to be a quadratic expression in the **variable** x, with a, b and c representing **constants**. Of course, the values of a, b and c change from one quadratic to another.

How does an identity differ from an equation?

An identity is true for **any** value of the variable. An equation is only true for specific values of the variable, these values being called the solutions of the equation.

EXERCISE 1

1 (a) $x = -3$ (b) $x = \pm 5$ (c) $x = -6, 1$
   (d) $x = \pm 2$ (e) $x = 0$ (f) $x = 0, 4$

2 (a) $1 + 2 + \ldots + n = 210$

$$\tfrac{1}{2}n(n + 1) = 210$$

$$n^2 + n - 420 = 0$$

(b) $(n - 20)(n + 21) = 0$

$$n = 20 \text{ (choosing the positive root)}$$

4.2 Quadratic equations

E X E R C I S E 2

1 (i) $\dfrac{-5 \pm \sqrt{13}}{2} = -4.30 \text{ or } -0.70$ (ii) $\dfrac{-6 \pm \sqrt{12}}{6} = 1.58 \text{ or } -0.42$

(iii) $\dfrac{-4 \pm \sqrt{28}}{6} = -1.55 \text{ or } 0.22$ (iv) $\dfrac{8 \pm \sqrt{84}}{10} = -0.12 \text{ or } 1.72$

(v) $\dfrac{7 \pm \sqrt{57}}{4} = -0.14 \text{ or } 3.64$

2 (a) $x^2 + 2x - 4 = 0 \Rightarrow x = -3.24 \text{ or } 1.24$

(b) $5x^2 - 3x - 4 = 0 \Rightarrow x = -0.64 \text{ or } 1.24$

(c) 1.44 or 5.56

(d) –0.84 or 0.24

3 (a) 0, 8   (b) –1, 4   (c) –1.62, 0.62

(d) $x = \pm 5$ (e) no solutions   (f) 5

4 (a) Area of path $= x \times 1 + (3x + 2) \times 1 + x \times 1 = 5x + 2$

Area of lawn $= 3x \times x = 3x^2 \Rightarrow 3x^2 = 5x + 2$

(b) $3x^2 - 5x - 2 = 0 \Rightarrow x = 2$ since x must be positive.

The dimensions are 2 metres × 6 metres.

5 (a) The numbers are n and $n + 1$. Therefore $n(n + 1) = 10$

(b) $n = \dfrac{-1 \pm \sqrt{41}}{2} = 2.7 \text{ or } -3.7$ to 1 d.p.

6 (a) (i) no solutions   (ii) $x = 2$ (iii) 0.76, 5.24

(b) From left to right, the graphs are for (i), (iii), (ii).

(c) If $b^2 - 4ac < 0$, the equation has no solutions.

If $b^2 - 4ac = 0$, the equation has a single (repeated) solution.

If $b^2 - 4ac > 0$, the equation has two solutions.

4.3 Inequalities

> What is the first triangular number greater than 50?

The solution is given in the text.

> What is meant by a solution set?

All the values which solve the problem are said to form the solution set. If there are no such values the solution set is said to be empty.

> By sketching an appropriate graph, solve the cubic inequality
>
> $(x + 1)(x - 2)(x - 4) \leq 0$

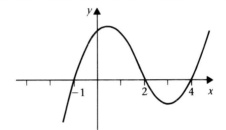

The solution set is $x \leq -1$ or $2 \leq x \leq 4$.

E X E R C I S E   3

1 (a) $x < -2$ (b) $-5 < 5x \Rightarrow -1 < x$ (c) $2x - 6 < 8 \Rightarrow x < 7$
  (d) $3x + 15 < 2x + 3 \Rightarrow x < -12$ (e) $x > -2$

2 The square of any number except 0 is positive. Therefore x may take any value except 2.

3 (a) $-3 \leq x \leq 1$ (b) $x < -4$ or $x > 2$ (c) $-2 < x < 2$

4 (a) $x < -5$ or $x > 2$ (b) $x \leq 2$ or $x \geq 3$
  (c) $-2 \leq x \leq 2$ or $x \geq 5$ (d) $x \geq -2$

5 (a) $0 < x < 3$ (b) $0 \leq x \leq 1$

  (c) $-2 < x < 5$ (d) $x < \dfrac{-1 - \sqrt{5}}{2}$ or $x > \dfrac{-1 + \sqrt{5}}{2}$

6 $\dfrac{n^2 + n}{2} > 1000 \Rightarrow n^2 + n - 2000 > 0 \quad n = 45$

4.4 Polynomials

> Check that $(x + 1)(x - 2)(x + 4) = x^3 + 3x^2 - 6x - 8$

$$(x + 1)(x - 2)(x + 4) = (x^2 - x - 2)(x + 4)$$
$$= x^3 - x^2 - 2x$$
$$+ 4x^2 - 4x - 8$$
$$= x^3 + 3x^2 - 6x - 8$$

If you are not confident about performing such expansions, tasksheet 5S is designed to help you.

E X E R C I S E 4

1 (a) $P(-3) = 0$ (b) $Q(x) = x^2 - 5x + 4$

2 (a) $P(-1) = 0 \Rightarrow x + 1$ is a factor   (b) $(x + 1)(x - 2)(x - 4)$

   (c) $-1, 2, 4$ (d)

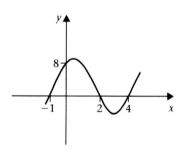

3 $1, -3$

4 $(x + 2)(x^2 + 2x - 2) = 0$

   $\Rightarrow x = -2, 0.73, -2.73$

5 (a) $(x + 2)(x^2 - 2x + 2) = 0$ (b)

   $\Rightarrow x = -2$

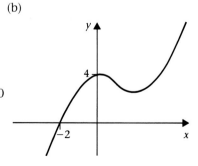

The quadratic equation $x^2 - 2x + 2 = 0$ has no solutions, hence the cubic equation has only one solution.

6 (a) Zeros are –2, –1, 1 and 3.

   $P(x) = (x - 3)(x - 1)(x + 1)(x + 2)$

(b)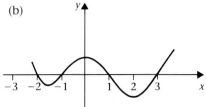

(c) $x < -2$ or $-1 < x < 1$ or $x > 3$

7 (a) (i) $x^3 - 8 = (x - 2)(x^2 + 2x + 4)$ (ii) $x^4 - 16 = (x^2 + 4)(x - 2)(x + 2)$

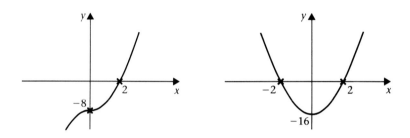

Each linear factor gives rise to a zero. Quadratic factors which cannot be factorised contribute no further zeros.

5 Numerical methods

5.2 Locating roots

E X E R C I S E 1

1 (a) The interval [3, 4]

  (b) $x = 1$ is one root; the other two lie in $[-1, 0]$ and $[-4, -3]$.

  (c) [1, 2]   (d) $[-3, -2]$, [2, 3]

2 (a) 3.14   (b) –3.41, –0.59, 1   (c) 1.72   (d) –2.32, 2.32

5.3   Iterative formulas

E X E R C I S E   2

1   (a)   (i) $x^3 = 10 \Rightarrow x^2 = \dfrac{10}{x} \Rightarrow x = \sqrt{\dfrac{10}{x}}$

   (ii) $x_1 = 2$, $x_2 = 2.236067977$, $x = 2.15443$ to 5 d.p.

   (b)   (i) $x^3 = 10 \Rightarrow x^4 = 10x \Rightarrow x^2 = \sqrt{10x} \Rightarrow x = \sqrt{\sqrt{10x}}$

   (ii) $x_1 = 2$, $x_2 = 2.114742527$, $x = 2.15443$ to 5 d.p.

   In part (b) the convergence to the solution is much faster.

2   Using the iterative formula $x_{i+1} = \dfrac{1}{3}(2^{x_i})$

   $x_1 = 3$
   $x_2 = 2.\dot{6}$
   $x = 0.4578$ to 4 d.p.

3   (a)   [3, 4]

   (b) $x^2 - 1 = 6\sqrt{x}$

   $\Rightarrow x^2 = 6\sqrt{x} + 1$

   $\Rightarrow x = \sqrt{6\sqrt{x} + 1}$

   (c)   With $x_1 = 3$, $x_2 = 3.37525$ and $x = 3.495358$ to 6 d.p.

4   (b) $x^3 + 2x - 1 = 0$

   $\Rightarrow 2x = 1 - x^3$

   $\Rightarrow x = \dfrac{1}{2}(1 - x^3)$

   (c)   (i) 0.45340   (ii) 0.45340

   (d) $x_1 = 2$ gives $x_2 = -3.5$, $x_3 = 21.9$, $x_4 = -5278$.

   The sequence diverges and $x_1 = 2$ is clearly an unsuitable starting value.

5 (b) (ii) $x_1 = 0$ would give $\sqrt{\dfrac{-1}{2}}$ which cannot be found.

(ii) $x_1 = 1$ gives 2.280776 after 27 iterations

$x_1 = 2$ gives 2.280776 after 24 iterations

$x_1 = 10$ gives 2.280776 after 30 iterations.

(c) $x_1 = 1$ gives 2.280776 after 8 iterations

$x_1 = 2$ gives 2.280776 after 7 iterations

$x_1 = 10$ gives 2.280776 after 10 iterations.

(d) $x_1 = 1$ gives 2.219224 after 11 iterations

$x_1 = 2$ gives 2.219224 after 14 iterations

$x_1 = 3$ diverges.

(e) The iterations in (b) and (c) converge to the root in the interval [2, 3] but not to the root in [0, 1], even with a starting value of 1.

The convergence of (b) is very slow.

The iteration in (d) will converge to the root in [0, 1] but not to the one in [2, 3].